Perceptual Quotes for
Photographers

Perceptual Quotes for Photographers

Richard D. Zakia

LIGHT IMPRESSIONS CORPORATION
Rochester, New York

Books by Richard D. Zakia

VISUAL CONCEPTS FOR PHOTOGRAPHERS
1980 (with Les Stroebel and Hollis Todd)

NEW ZONE SYSTEM MANUAL
1976 (with Minor White and Peter Lorenz)

PERCEPTION AND PHOTOGRAPHY
1975

COLOR PRIMER I AND II
1974 (with Hollis Todd)

ZONE SYSTEMIZER
1973 (with John Dowdell)

101 EXPERIMENTS IN PHOTOGRAPHY
1969 (with Hollis Todd)

PHOTOGRAPHIC SENSITOMETRY
1969 (with Hollis Todd)

ISBN 0-87992-019-X
Copyright © 1980 Richard D. Zakia
Printed in the United States of America

Library of Congress Cataloging in Publication Data

Perceptual quotes for photographers.

    Bibliography: p.
    Includes index.
    1. Visual perception--Quotations, maxims, etc.
I. Zakia, Richard D.
PN6084.V58P4   701'.1'5   80-15008
ISBN 0-87992-019-X

Dedicated to the verbal artists of the world,
past and present and especially
to Minor White
who as an artist
was both visual and verbal.

Contents

As long as I can remember I have been a collector of quotations. For the past several years I have been very much interested in perception and how it relates to photography. This book, then, encompasses both of my interests, and is something that has evolved quite naturally. For me these selected quotations represent verbal images and this book, a gallery for displaying them. The book is an invitation to the reader to view the images, beginning wherever his interest directs him, taking as long as he wants and returning as often as he desires. As with any gallery the reader will find some images more appealing than others.

Does the book have a theme? This is the question Minor White asked when he first read my initial draft in 1975. Perhaps the table of contents suggests one. Perception, like a diamond, has many facets, each of which is an integral part of the whole. Man displays many facets; images come to us from all over, from without and from within, and are woven by the fabric of the mind to leave traces in memory. Perception provides us with experiences through the mingling of what is out there and what is within us. The form these images take matters little and all are in some sense, equivalent. The more we tune in to the multiple facets of potential imagery, the more sensitive we become and the richer are our images and experiences. **Perceptual Quotes For Photographers** is my attempt to heighten awareness of one facet of imagery — verbal imagery.

Ben Shahn's quote, which follows, eloquently testifies to the fact that all imagery is imagery regardless of where it originates and how it is processed:

> *"I daresay that some hypothetical artist, asked to put forth a theory of knowledge, would promptly reply that all knowledge exists in the form of images. He would imply not only visual*

images, nor only symbolic images; he would mean as well the many other sensory images — touch, taste, hearing, pain, and so on; the images of emotional states; of complicated intellectual experience; motor images; the combined and compounded images that involve senses, mind, and emotions all at once. He would probably regard behavior patterns as imagery, and certainly language, both written and spoken. Thinking, according to his view would consist in the marshalling of appropriate images toward an implied end. And knowledge itself is an awareness and an ability to invoke all manner of images at will."

A line in an Alaskan Eskimo song reads, *"My whole body is covered with eyes: Behold it!"*

Although many writers and authors have been quoted in this book, many more could have been. I have simply used books with which I am familiar and which are on my bookshelf. Few photographers have been included in order to encourage photographers to search beyond the writings in their own discipline for ideas and inspiration. The quotes are put into perceptual categories for convenience only. Some could have been put easily into more than one category; all are related and present but a facet of the perceptual diamond. Through juxtaposition, the quotes by persons in various disciplines from different times work together in a new context to form a verbal collage. For convenience again, the quotes in each category are listed alphabetically according to author. I have tried my best to sustain the integrity of each statement so that it would not lose its intent as it is removed from one context and put into another.

I extend my sincere gratitude to the authors and publishers whose work made this book possible: to George De Wolfe and to Lois Zakia who have helped and encouraged me from the very beginning; to my former students, Charlotte Marine and Don Harbison, who gave so generously of their time and talents; to Nate Lyons for sharing his thoughts on perception with me; and to Ralph Hattersley for his continued encouragement.

May you enjoy what I have compiled, share it with your friends and return to it often.

Richard D. Zakia
Rochester, New York

In a sense we see with words. That is, we tend to see only what we are looking for and generally restrict ourselves to those things for which we have names. Things that are unnamed go unseen and unremembered. Since words are so important in seeing it is only reasonable that we should have words concerning the process of seeing itself. This book provides us with an abundance of them — simple words applied to the context of seeing. These words can help us keep track of what we are actually doing when we look at something. Otherwise, the visual process is more or less a mystery.

When vision itself is a mystery many of its wonders go unobserved. It becomes an automatic process of which we are only vaguely aware. We know that we see — any idiot knows this — but the question of how we see is left in limbo. However, the how we do it of seeing is a fascinating subject with an endless number of puzzling aspects, and understanding it can provide a lifetime goal. **Perceptual Quotes for Photographers** gives us a handy framework for this understanding by dividing visual perception into many of its aspects so that we can see them better. It also helps us see them all as a whole: human visual perception.

The quotes in this book are all short, but they are also very dense. That is, information and ideas are packed very tightly into them, with no loose or wasted space. Thus unpacking such a tightly wrought paragraph is a special problem best solved by a form of meditation. The thing to do is to seize onto a quotation and meditate on it until its meaning becomes clear. You may be sure that it will be worth your time and effort, for these are very beautifully contrived quotations. Indeed they contain the wisdom of ages, all laid out in the simplest way for your examination.

Richard Zakia tells us that these quotes are for photographers, though they could just as well be for all those who are involved anywhere in the visual arts and even for those who are simply curious about visual perception. However, he has long had an interest in photographers as an educator and has made this collection especially for them. As a rule they are people greatly interested in seeing. Zakia tells them, "Take your interest one step further: examine the inner nature of vision as such. Learn what visual perception is all about."

Essentially, he is telling photographers to observe themselves as observers and in that way come to understand why they see the way they do. With that understanding will come an expansion of the individual's personal world. When you have more things to look for there will be more that you see. In observing yourself as an observer you can greatly intensify your awareness of things. You can turn a spotlight on your personal world and the outside world at the same time.

The Table of Contents is especially interesting, for it reveals the great care and understanding with which Zakia has organized his quotations. It clearly shows the framework around which the book is constructed and can serve as a condensed description of the nature of visual perception. Use this table as a study guide, because it is admirably adapted for this purpose. Use it to test your awareness of your own visual perception. Do you personally understand all the terms? If not you still have a way to go.

You can treat this book as a novel and read it straight through from beginning to end. When you first approach the quotes this is a good idea — it will tell you what is available for you. Thereafter it might be better to just dip in here and there, using the Table of Contents as a guide. Often you should find just one suitable quote to meditate on, then stick with it until the meaning has become very clear. It seems obvious that the author intends for you to get a lot of mileage out of each entry, so it would be wise to go along with him.

Photographers traditionally like to talk about photography, but they often get hung up on technique and can't think of anything else to dwell on. Richard Zakia's book provides a whole raft of new things to talk about in the context of photography. Though the quotes often fail to mention photography as such, a connection can be made by the intelligent reader who is willing to try. Actually, every single one of them can be seen as applying directly to photography as a process involving visual perception.

The quotations in this work are deceptively simple, but don't let this fool you. Nearly every one of them could be expanded into a whole chapter — you might try doing this on your own. And taken together they add up to a statement concerning visual perception that is complex enough for anyone. Zakia kind of creeps up on you, so that by the time you have finished the book you find that you have been taken on a real trip. His technique is to use simplicity to lead the reader into complexity without frightening him. In truth, visual perception is extremely complex, but that is not reason for being afraid of it as a field of study. If you build onto your understanding brick by brick you will eventually accomplish much.

A few words concerning your author would be appropriate here. He is a man both courteous and kind who has worked for many years with photography students and teachers at the Rochester Institute of Technology. He himself is a photographer, a photographic scientist, and an educator. As a teacher he is especially concerned with language and uses it with great care — his selection of quotations shows this. He believes that good communication is the very core of the learning process and that it must involve the teacher deeply caring for students. His biggest challenge is to help his students make sense out of the world they live in. In this all-important area he is especially good. As a teacher he is one of those rare individuals who can actually explain what he means in an understandable way.

Ralph Hattersley
Virginia Beach, VA

James Agee
Aristotle
Rudolf Arnheim
Marcus Aurelius
Bernard Berenson
Ray Birdwhistell
William Blake
T.G.R. Bower
Henri Cartier Bresson
Jerome Bruner
Barbara Bullock-Wilson
Robert Burns
Albert Camus
Cornell Capa
Fritjof Capra
Edmund Carpenter
Paul Cezanne
Winston Churchill
Graham Collier
Democritus
John Dewey
Neil Diamond
N.F. Dixon
Rene Dubos
Albrecht Durer
Ecclesiastes
Loren Eisley
Ralph Waldo Emerson
Ralph Evans

Walker Evans
Leon Festinger
Rasheed bin Fouad
Viktor Frankl
Sigmund Freud
Erich Fromm
R. Buckminster Fuller
Kahlil Gibran
James Gibson
E.H. Gombrich
Andrew Greeley
Richard Gregory
Gertrud Grunow
Ralph Norman Haber
Calvin Hall
Edward Hall
Dag Hammarskjold
Sidney Harris
Nathaniel Hawthorne
Werner Heisenberg
Hermann Helmholtz
Heraclitus
Walter Hilton
Alfred Hitchcock
William Ittelson
Henry James
William James
Carl Jung
Joseph Kerwin

Wilson Bryan Key
Omar Khayyam
Rudyard Kipling
Paul Klee
Arthur Koestler
Kurt Koffka
Wolfgang Kohler
Lao Tze
D.H. Lawrence
Gottfried Wilheim
  Leibnitz
Henry Wadsworth
  Longfellow
Ernst Mach
Thomas Mann
Norman Mailer
Abraham Maslow
Rollo May
Marshall McLuhan
Joost Meerloo
Thomas Merton
George Miller
Ashley Montagu
Desmond Morris
Ulric Neisser
Robert Ornstein
Harley Parker
Louis Pasteur
Jean Piaget
Pablo Picasso
Max Planck

Pope John XXIII
Floyd Ratliff
Carl Rogers
Eleanor Roosevelt
John Ruskin
Antoine de
  Saint Exupery
Edward Sapir
Arthur Schopenhauer
Ben Shahn
William Shakespeare
George Bernard Shaw
Percy Bysshe Shelley
Viktor Shklovsky
Susan Sontag
Rene Spitz
Teilhard de Chardin
St. Thomas
Harry Stack Sullivan
Henry Thoreau
Leo Tolstoy
Jerry Uelsmann
Richard Wagner
Richard and Roslyn
  Warren
Minor White
John Whittier
William Wordsworth
Thomas Wolfe
William Butler Yeats

In looking at an object we reach out for it. With
an invisible finger we move through the space
around us, go out to the distant places where
things are found, touch them, catch them, scan
their surfaces, trace their borders, explore their
texture. It is an eminently active occupation.

Rudolf Arnheim

The perceiver is not seen as a passive and in-
different organism but rather as one who actively
selects information, forms perceptual hypotheses,
and on occasion distorts the input in the service of
reducing surprise and of attaining valued objects.

Jerome Bruner

We shall have to conceive the external senses in a
new way, as active rather than passive, as systems
rather than channels, and as interrelated rather
than mutually exclusive. If they function to pick
up information, not simply to arouse sensations,
this function should be denoted by a different
term. They will here be called perceptual systems.

James Gibson

The eye is less efficient when the observer is
carried passively, in a car or plane, than when
information of movement is available through the
limbs in contact with the earth.

Richard Gregory

Man actively though unconsciously structures his
visual world. Few people realize that vision is not
passive but active, in fact, a transaction between

1

Perception Is Active

Edward Hall

man and his environment in which both participate.

Ulric Neisser

In normal use the eyes are rarely still for long. Apart from small tremors, their most common movement is the flick from one position to another called a "saccade." Saccades usually take less than a twentieth of a second, but they happen several times each second in reading and may be just as frequent when a picture or an actual scene is being inspected. This means that there is a new retinal image every few hundred milliseconds.

Minor White

In putting images together I become active, and excitement is of another order — synthesis overshadows analysis.

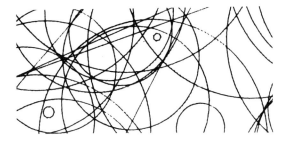

The photographs are not illustrative. They, and the text, are coequal, mutually independent, and fully collaborative. By their fewness, and by the impotance of the reader's eye, this will be misunderstood by most of that minority which does not wholly ignore it. In the interests, however, of the history and future of photography, that risk seems irrelevant, and this flat statement necessary.

James Agee and Walker Evans

When the image of an object changes, the observer must know whether the change is due to the object itself or to the context or to both, otherwise he understands neither the object nor its surroundings. Intertwined though the two appear, one can attempt to tease them apart, especially by watching the same object in different contexts and the same context acting on different objects.

Rudolf Arnheim

... gestures not only do not stand alone as behavioral isolates but they also do not have explicit and invariable meanings.... By the study of gestures in context, it became clear that the kinesic system has forms which are astonishingly like words in language.

Ray Birdwhistell

The sense organs receive patterns of energy, but we seldom see patterns: we see objects. A pattern

3

Perception Is Contextual

is a relatively meaningless arrangement of marks, but objects have a host of characteristics beyond their sensory features. They have pasts and futures; they change and influence each other, and have hidden aspects which emerge under different

Richard Gregory   conditions.

Every with, by, above, below, behind interrelation in the living interchange of forces is based on a special, lawful inner order and evokes a particular

Gertrud Grunow   sensation and an external appearance.

Every organism lives out its day in relation to, and as part of, a larger environmental context. All but the most primitive organisms receive information from this context through sense organs and process it, together with information from other sources,

William Ittelson   in a nervous system.

Mental facts cannot be properly studied apart from the physical environment in which they take

William James   cognizance.

The artist of today is more than an improved camera, he is more complex, richer, and wider. He is a creature on the earth and a creature within the

Paul Klee   whole, that is, a creature on a star among stars.

To engage a sequence we keep in mind the

Minor White   photographs on either side of the one in our eye.

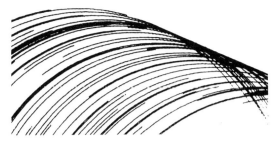

There is considerable evidence to indicate that the graspability of shapes and colors varies, depending on the species, the cultural group, the amount of training of the observer. What is rational for one group, will be irrational for another, i.e., it cannot be grasped, understood, compared, or remembered.

Rudolf Arnheim

The formula used for the preparation of Coca-Cola, I understand, is not quite the same in New York as it is in New Orleans, in Vermont as in Virginia.

Rene Dubos

No man can quite emancipate himself from his age and country, or produce a model in which the education, the religion, the politics, usages and arts of his times shall have no share.

Ralph Waldo Emerson

The vast majority of people in our culture are well adjusted because they have given up the battle for independence sooner and more radically than the neurotic person. They have accepted the judgment of the majority so completely that they have been spared the sharp pain of conflict which the neurotic person goes through.

Erich Fromm

...no matter how hard man tries it is impossible for him to divest himself of his own culture, for it

Perception Is Cultural

Edward Hall

has penetrated to the roots of his nervous system and determines how he perceives the world.

Ashley Montagu

There are whole cultures which are characterized by a *"Noli mi tangere,"* a "Do not touch me," way of life. There are other cultures in which tactility is so much a part of life, in which there is so much embracing and fondling and kissing it appears strange and embarrassing to the non-tactile peoples. And there are cultures that play every possible variation upon the theme of tactility.

Harry Stack Sullivan

The cultural entities, so to speak, are part of the necessary environment. The human being requires the world of culture, cannot live *and be human* except in communal existance with it. The world of culture is, however, clearly manifest only in human behavior and thought. Other people are, therefore, an indispensable part of the environment of the human organism.

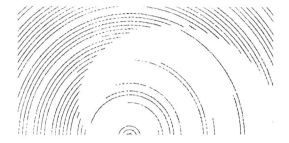

...in man there is a primitive unity of the senses,
with visual variables specifying tactile consequences; further, this primitive unity is built into
the structure of the human nervous system.

T.G.R. Bower

...certain primitive unities or identities within
perception must be innate or autochthonous and
not learned. The primitive capacity to categorize
things from background is very likely one such;
and so, too, the capacity to distinguish events in
one modality from those in others — although the
phenomena of synesthesia would suggest that this
is not so complete a juncture as it might seem.

Jerome Bruner

Modern man retains the same potentialities for
keenness of perception that his distant ancestors
had, as demonstrated by the fact that persons who
have removed themselves from technicalized
environments commonly display increased ability
to perceive colors, sounds and odors.

Rene Dubos

The anatomy and basic physiology of the organs
of perception depend mainly on genetic factors as
determined by evolution. The maturation of
perceptual systems depends on genetic and environmental determiners in concert.

James Gibson

Whatever the fate of the Gestalt school may be in
the field of neurology, it may still prove logically

Perception Is Innate

E.H. Gombrich right in insisting that the simplicity hypothesis cannot be learned.

Abraham Maslow We have, each of us, an essential biologically based inner nature, which is to some degree "natural," intrinsic, given, and, in a certain limited sense, unchangeable, or, at least, unchanging.

Joost Meerloo ...in the dance man's earliest existence is revealed, rhythm and gesture somewhere reverberate man's nirvanic yearning. Whenever rhythm, cadence, syncopation reach ear and eye man is unobtrusively dragged back into the very beginning of his existence; together with others he undergoes a regression.

Jean Piaget In short, the learning of any structures seems itself to include a logic inherent to its functioning, comparable at the beginning to this prelogic already at play in perception, then tending to join the inductive and deductive structures which finally supply learning as such.

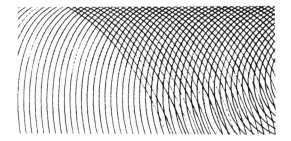

This is a *book* only by necessity. More seriously,
it is an effort in human actuality, in which the
reader is no less centrally involved than the
authors and those of whom they tell.

*James Agee and
Walker Evans*

Places and persons acquire their distinctiveness
from the interplay between their inherent
characteristics and the external forces that act
upon them.

Rene Dubos

...man learns while he sees and what he learns
influences what he sees.

Edward Hall

Whilst part of what we perceive comes through
our senses from the object before us, another part
(and it may be the larger part) aways comes out of
our own mind.

William James

...color contrast had naturally to be regarded as
further proof that the properties of local facts are
affected by the conditions present in their environment, in other words, that interaction takes
place in the perceptual field.

Wolfgang Kohler

Yet with great sophistication the quantum theory
also accounts for the 'factual' concepts of everyday
life, knowing that they are to be taken into account as part of the observer's reality; and this

Perception Is Interactive

destroys the myth of the completely separate and detached observer... The observer is part of the observed. We are part of nature and our knowledge of nature is nothing if not knowledge of nature as known by us, who are parts of it.

Thomas Merton

Idea itself — ideas, many ideas move back and forth across his mind as a constant traffic, dominated perhaps by larger currents and directions, by what he wants to think. Thus idea rises to the surface, grows, changes as a painting grows and develops. So one must say that painting is both creative and responsive. It is an intimately communicative affair between the painter and his painting, a conversation back and forth, the painting telling the painter even as it receives its shape and form.

Ben Shahn

I have gradually confused photography and life and as a result of this I believe I am able to work out of myself at an almost precognitive level.

Jerry Uelsmann

As I become more in harmony with the world around, through, and in me, the varieties of time weave together.

Minor White

Perception Is Learned

The artist has his idea in a flash. What the flash
will present or reveal is a result not only of the
gifts that he brought with him at birth, but of all
that he has absorbed from his surroundings and
experience: from his conditioning, his education,
his parents, his companions, his love affairs,
reading, and travels — in short, his entire
existence.   *Bernard Berenson*

Gregory Bateson...points out that human learning
is patterned, that we learn to learn, that we learn
to learn to learn, and that we also learn to learn
not to learn.   *Ray Birdwhistell*

Interpreting photographs is an important skill that
must be learned by all who have to deal with this
medium of communication: the intelligence officer,
the surveyor or archaeologist who studies aerial
photographs, the sports photographer who wishes
to record and to judge athletic events and the
physician who reads X-ray plates.   *E.H. Gombrich*

We think of perception as an active process of
using information to suggest and test hypotheses.
Clearly this involves learning, and whatever the
final answer on the importance of perceptual
learning in babies, it does seem clear that
knowledge of non-visual characteristics affects how
objects are seen.   *Richard Gregory*

Perception Is Learned

Edward Hall

People reared in different cultures *learn to learn* differently. Some do so by memory and rote without reference to "logic"...some by demonstration. Some cultures, like the American, stress doing as a principle of learning, while others have very little of the pragmatic.

Hermann Helmholtz

For apprehension by the senses supplies after all, directly or indirectly, the material of all human knowledge, or at least the stimulus necessary to develop every inborn faculty of the mind.

William James

The one who *thinks* over his experiences most, and weaves them into systematic relations with each other, will be the one with the best memory.

Rudyard Kipling

There aren't twelve hundred people in the world who understand pictures. The others pretend and don't care.

Rene Spitz

...perception has to be learned, coordinated, integrated, and synthesized through experiencing the unceasing and shifting tides, the quite pools, the rapids of object relations.

Under natural conditions, vision has to cope with more than one or two objects at a time. More often than not, the visual field is overcrowded and does not submit to an integrated organization of the whole. In a typical life situation, a person concentrates on some selected areas and items or on some overall features while the structure of the remainder is sketchy and loose.

Rudolf Arnheim

If the doors of perception were cleansed, man would see everything as it is, infinite.

William Blake

Of the total electro-mechanical spectrum range of the now known realities of Universe, man has the sensory equipment to tune in directly with but one-millionth of the thus far discovered physical Universe events.

R. Buckminster Fuller

The capacity of memory for pictures may be unlimited. Common experience suggests that this is so. For example, almost everyone has had the experience of recognizing a face he saw only briefly years before.

Ralph Haber

...environments always provide more information than can possibly be processed. Questions of channel capacity and overload are inherent to environmental studies. However, the mere quantity of information does not tell the whole

Perception Is Limtied

William Ittelson

story. Environments always represent simultaneously, instances of redundant information, of inadequate and ambiguous information, and of conflicting and contradictory information.

Carl Jung

...consciousness can keep only a few images in full clarity at one time, and even this clarity fluctuates.

George Miller

We are able to perceive up to about six dots accurately without counting; beyond this errors become frequent.

Robert Ornstein

All humans may agree on certain events only because we are all similarly limited in our very structure as well as limited in our culture.

Arthur Schopenhauer

Every man takes the limits of his own field of vision for the limits of the world.

When looking at a human figure, a sculptor forms
a representational concept very different from the
one of another artist who looks at the same figure
with 'woodcut-eyes.'

Rudolf Arnheim

Bullock saw clearly that in order to maximize a
photograph's potential, a photographer has be
aware of his own functioning. The greater a
photographer's awareness, the greater his ability to
function more effectively and the greater his
photograph's potential to symbolize meaning.

*Barbara Bullock-
Wilson*

Oh wad some power the giftie gie us
To see oursels as others see us!
It wad frae monie a blunder free us,
An' foolish notion.

Robert Burns

The idea that any photography can't be personal is
madness! ... I see something; it goes through my
eye, brain, heart, guts; I choose the subject. What
could be more personal than that?

Cornell Capa

As I am, so I see; use what language we will, we
can never say anything but what we are.

*Ralph Waldo
Emerson*

Any point of view is interesting that is a direct
impression of life. You each have an impression
coloured by your individual conditions; make that

Henry James   into a picture, a picture framed by your own personal wisdom, your glimpse of the American world.

Wolfgang Kohler   But external objects cannot *present* moods and emotions. Emotions and moods are inside the person who has them, not outside.

Henry Thoreau   How differently the poet and the naturalist look at objects! A man sees only what concerns him. A botanist absorbed in the pursuit of grasses does not distinguish the grandest pasture oaks. He as it were tramples down oaks unwittingly in his walk.

Ben Shahn   Only an individual can imagine, invent or create. The whole audience of art is an audience of individuals.

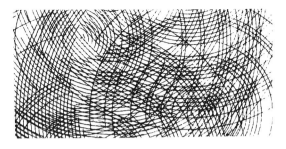

Through that world roams the glance, directed by attention, focusing the narrow range of sharpest vision now on this, now on that spot, following the flight of a distant sea gull, scanning a tree to explore its shape. This eminently active performance is what is truly meant by visual perception. It may refer to a small part of the visual world or to the whole visual framework of space in which all presently seen objects have their location. The world emerging from this perceptual exploration is not immediately given.

Rudolf Arnheim

Let me summarize our considerations about the general properties of perception with a few propositions. The first is that perception is a decision process. Whatever the nature of the task set, the perceiver or his nervous system decides that a thing perceived is one thing and not another. A line is longer or shorter than a standard, a particular object is a snake and not a fallen branch, the incomplete word *l*ve* in the context men l*ve women is the word *love* not *live*.

Jerome Bruner

Nature, as I have tried to intimate, is never quite where we see it. It is a becoming as well as a passing, but the becoming is both within and without our power.

Loren Eisley

...the memory process can be regarded as a system

17

Perception Is A Process

Ralph Haber

concerned with information processing that consists of several stages and has its own time constants for extraction, decay, mode of persistence, susceptibility to interference or erasure, and the like.

William Ittelson

Affect, orientation, categorization, systemization, and manipulation are the processes involved in environment perception. They do not function sequentially, but continuously interact with each other. Each aspect calls for its own set of strategies which are probably characteristic of the individual.

William James

Consciousness, then, does not appear to itself chopped up in bits. Such words as 'chain' or 'train' do not describe it fitly as it presents itself in the first instance. It is nothing jointed; it flows. A 'river' or a 'stream' are the metaphors by which it is most naturally described. In talking of it hereafter, let us call it the stream of thought, of consciousness, or of subjective life.

Ben Shahn

The moving toward one's inner self is a long pilgrimage for a painter. It offers many temporary successes and high points, but there is always the residuum of incomplete realization which impels him on toward the more adequate image.

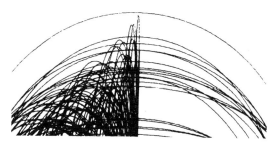

The perceived brightness of, say, a piece of paper
is derived from its place on the scale of brightness
that reaches from the brightest to the darkest value
visible in the field. What is being received is not
an absolute but a relative value.

Rudolf Arnheim

In the perception of the spatial field as a whole, all
distances are fixed primarily with reference to the
position of the body, and, secondarily, with
reference to each other. It is, in fact, the mutual
reference of objects to each other that makes
perception accurate and complete.

John Dewey

When at night I look at the moon and stars, I
seem stationary, and they to hurry.

*Ralph Waldo
Emerson*

One man's justice is another's injustice; one man's
beauty another's ugliness; one man's wisdom
another's folly; as one beholds the same objects
from a higher point.

*Ralph Waldo
Emerson*

All works of art are created on a certain scale.
Altering the size alters everything.

Edward Hall

The simple rule for all illusions of sight is this: *we
always believe that we see such objects as would,
under conditions of normal vision, produce the
retinal image of which we are actually conscious.*
If these images are such as could not be produced

Perception Is Relative

Hermann
Helmholtz
by any normal kind of observation, we judge of them according to their nearest resemblance.

Wolfgang Kohler
Take color vision: when a gray object surrounded by a white surface is compared with a second object that, physically, has the same gray color but is surrounded by a black surface, the gray-on-white object looks darker than the gray-on-black object.

Ben Shahn
...consider Van Gogh; to the psychologist it is the periodic insanity of Van Gogh that is pre-eminent, and the psychologist deduces much from that. But to the artist it is clear that it was the great love of things and of people and the incredible suffering of Van Gogh that made his art possible and his insanity inevitable.

Henry Thoreau
When the far mountains are invisble, the near ones look the higher.

Henry Thoreau
I am always struck by the centrality of the observer's position. He always stands fronting the middle of the arch, and does not suspect at first that a thousand observers on a thousand hills behold the sunset sky from equally favorable positions.

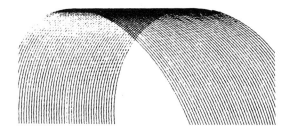

In order to interpret the functioning of the senses properly, one needs to keep in mind that they ... evolved as biological aids for survival. From the beginning they aimed at, and concentrated on, those features of the surroundings that made the difference between the enhancement and the impediment of life. This means that perception is purposive and selective.

Rudolf Arnheim

Sensory information can by-pass awareness, either because it is subliminal ... or because some selective process in the subject results in exclusion from consciousness of part or parts of the total array.

N.F. Dixon

In exploratory looking, tasting, and touching the sense impressions are incidental symptoms of the exploration, and what gets isolated is information about the object looked at, tasted, or touched.

James Gibson

Consciousness is always interested more in one part of its object than in another, and welcomes and rejects, or chooses, all the while it thinks. ﹄

William James

The process of seeing is a process of abstraction, for in a very real sense the visual system schematizes and caricatures. From the immense detail in the retinal image the eye selects mainly that information which is of significance to the

Floyd Ratliff   organism, enhances it at the expense of less
significant information, and then transmits this
schema to the central nervous system.

Ben Shahn   To abstract is to draw out the essence of a matter.
To abstract in art is to separate certain fun-
damentals from irrelevant material which
surrounds them.

Teilhard de   It often happens that what stares us in the face is
Chardin   the most difficult to perceive.

Henry Thoreau   The question is not what you look at, but what
you see.

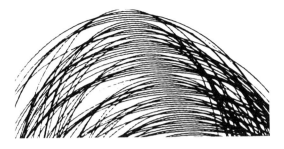

...as distance determines size, so size determines distance.

Rudolf Arnheim

It has been found that when vision and touch are put into conflict, vision invariably dominates.

T.G.R. Bower

Restraining sight increases awareness through other senses: in darkness, sounds seem louder, odors stronger, flavors sharper and surfaces more vivid.

Edmund Carpenter

"Come close that I may touch you, my son, to know whether you are really my son Esau or not." Jacob went close to his father; Issac touched him and said, "The voice is the voice of Jacob, but the hands are the hands of Esau."

Genesis 27:21

...whenever channel capacity is exceeded, temporal information is sacrificed in favor of retention of spatial characteristics.

Ralph Haber

In a word, to perceive an object abstractly means *not* to perceive some aspects of it. It clearly implies selection of some attributes, rejection of other attributes, creation or distortion of still others. We make of it what we wish. We create it.

Abraham Maslow

...the eye itself sacrifices accuracy about information of little consequence, such as the ab-

Perception Is A Trade-Off

solute levels of illumination, in order to enhance
features that are more significant, such as contours
and edges. The functional significance of inhibitory
interaction in the retina is at least partly to be
found in the roles it plays in the perservation and

Floyd Ratliff enhancement of this kind of information.

Is this a dagger which I see before me,
The handle toward my hand?
   Come, let me clutch thee:
I have thee not, and yet I see thee still.
Art thou not, fatal vision, sensible
To feeling as to sight? or art thou but

William A dagger of the mind, a false creation,
Shakespeare Proceeding from the heat-oppressed brain?

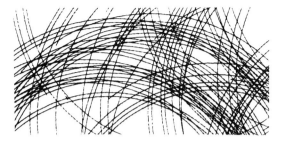

The changing appearance of a landscape or building in the morning, the evening, under electric light, with different weather and in different seasons offers two advantages. It presents an extraordinary richness of sight, and it tests the nature of the object by exposing it to varying conditions.

Rudolf Arnheim

What is there that we can exactly repeat, seeing that neither within nor without are we and our universe the same for two consecutive seconds?

Bernard Berenson

...just as there are no universal words, no sound complexes, which carry the same meaning the world over, there are no body motions, facial expressions or gestures which provoke *identical* response the world over.

Ray Birdwhistell

To the attentive eye, each moment of the year has its own beauty, and in the same field, it beholds, every hour, a picture which was never seen before and which shall never be seen again.

Ralph Waldo Emerson

In America linear perspective is still the more popular art style for the general public. Chinese and Japanese artists, on the other hand, symbolize depth in quite a different way. Oriental art shifts the viewing point while maintaining the scene as constant.

Edward Hall

Perception Is Variable

William James

We feel things differently accordingly as we are sleepy or awake, hungry or full, fresh or tired; differently at night and in the morning, differently in summer and in winter; and above all, differently in childhood, manhood, and old age.

Carl Jung

No individual symbolic image can be said to have a dogmatically fixed, generalized meaning.

Henry Thoreau

All distant landscapes seen from hilltops are veritable pictures, which will be found to have no actual existence to him who travels to them.

Rene Descartes has written, "I think, therefore I am." He could have also written, "I feel, therefore I am."

Rasheed bin Fouad

Another difficulty is that at moments of intense aesthetic experience we see not only with our eyes but with our whole body. The eyes scan, the cortex thinks, there are muscular stresses, innervations of the organs of touch, sensations of weight and temperature, visceral associations, feelings of rhythm and motion — all sucked into one integrated vortex.... The trouble with explaining visual beauty, and also its fascination, is that so much is happening at the same time.

Arthur Koestler

A landscape may seem tranquil, a mountain majestic, a melody sad because within the observer an incipient mood or emotion is aroused and then erroneously projected into the visual or auditory modalities. The melody itself cannot of course be sad, but the listener calls it that because he is unaware that his own viscera have discharged a tiny bit of sadness. He feels his way into what he hears.

Wolfgang Kohler

The skin belongs to the class of organs called *exteroceptors* because they pick up sensations from outside the body. Receptors that are stimulated principally by the actions of the body itself are

27

Perception Is Visceral

Ashley Montagu

called *proprioceptors.* It is both through its skin and the proprioceptors that the infant receives the messages from the muscle-joint-ligament behavior of the person holding it.

Antoine de Saint Exupery

It is only with the heart that one can see rightly; what is essential is invisible to the eye.

Ben Shahn

A fire is a cheerful affair. It is full of bright colors and moving shapes; it makes everybody happy. It is not your purpose to tell about a fire, not to describe a fire. Not at all; what you want to formulate is the terror, the heart-shaking fear. Now, find that image!

Harry Stack Sullivan

We learn in infancy that objects which our distance receptors, our eyes and ears for example, encounter, are of a quite different order of relationship from things which our tactile or our gustatory receptors encounter.

Henry Thoreau

A man has not seen a thing who has not felt it.

William Butler Yeats

God guard me from the thoughts men think
In the mind alone,
He that sings a lasting song
Thinks in a marrow bone.

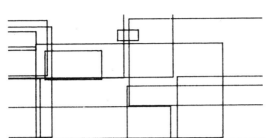

In looking at an object associations are not made
directly with the object but rather with stored
memory traces of the object.

*Rasheed bin
Fouad*

If various sensory elements, or even ideas, con-
tiguous in place or time, are associated
simultaneously in one activity, they become integral portions of it and recur with it.

John Dewey

When a person's verbal behavior is guided by
verbal stimuli of which he is unaware, he tends to
emit responses that are associations of these self-
same stimuli.

N.F. Dixon

...if techniques could be found to facilitate an
attaching of words to visual images, recall might
dramatically improve. Some people believe they
have this ability, for example, politicians who
seem to be able to associate a name with every
face they ever saw. Freud argued strongly that free
association was an ideal way to recover
irretrievable memories.

Ralph Haber

If ripening berries of a certain kind simultaneously
develop red pigment and sugar, in our perception
red color and sweet taste will always be found
together in berries of this kind.

*Hermann
Helmholtz*

The more other facts a fact is associated with in

William James

the mind, the better possession of it our memory retains.

Carl Jung

Every concept in our conscious mind, in short, has its own psychic associations. While such associations may vary in intensity ... they are capable of changing the "normal" character of that concept. It may even become something quite different as it drifts below the level of con- sciousness.

Arthur Koestler

When a painting is said to represent nothing but 'significant form' — to carry no meaning, associative connections, no reference to anything beyond itself — we can be confident that the speaker does not know what he is talking about. Neither the artist, nor the beholder of his work, can slice his mind into sections, separate sensation from perception, perception from meaning, sign from symbol.

Wolfgang Kohler

An association is often said to be a matter of contiguity, which means neighborhood of two items in space or time or both. We know that this condition, a short distance between objects, favors their unification in perception.

Minor White   Vision without association — pristine vision?

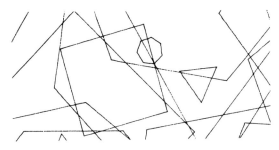

Words by which things are named are categories.
Such naming, therefore, indicates to some extent
the level of abstractions at which an object is
perceived and ought to be perceived.

Rudolf Arnheim

Western man is psycholinguistically dichotomous.
That is, he finds it comfortable, logical, and
reasonable to divide the universe into paired
categories like tall and short, good and bad, black
and white, and simple and complex.

Ray Birdwhistell

Perception involves an act of categorization ... we
stimulate an organism with some appropriate input
and he responds by referring the input to some
class of things or events ... The use of cues in
inferring the categorial identity of a perceived
object ... is as much a feature of perception as the
sensory stuff from which percepts are made.

Jerome Bruner

...failure to perceive is most often not a lack of
perceiving but a matter of interference with
perceiving. Whence the interference? I would
propose that the interference comes from
categorizations in highly accessible categories that
serve to block alternative categorizations in less
accessible categories.

Jerome Bruner

There are, of course, many more things in the
world than there are words in a language. Not

James Gibson

everything can be coded. The verbal responses, it is argued, must therefore categorize or cut up the real world in conventional ways that are necessarily inadequate to its full complexity.

E.H. Gombrich

Without categories, we could not sort our impressions. Paradoxically, it has turned out that it matters relatively little what these categories are. We can always adjust them according to need.

Hermann Helmholtz

For when "to comprehend" means to form concepts, and when we, in the concept of a class of objects, collect and summarize the characteristics which these objects have in common; it follows, in an entirely analogous manner, that the concept of a sequence of phenomena which changes with time must attempt to summarize that which remains the same in all stages.

William Ittelson

...conceptual categories are not imposed by the external situation, but are largely governed by goals, predispositions, and generalized expectations which the individual has already internalized. The path to unique and idosyncratic categories is open.

Robert Ornstein

As we mature, we attempt to make more and more consistent "sense" out of the mass of information arriving at our receptors. We develop stereotyped systems, or *categories,* for sorting input. The set of categories we develop is limited, much more limited than the input.

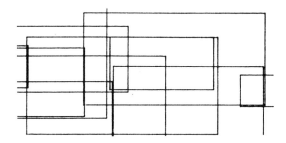

If the lighting in a scene is nonuniform or if there
are shadows, the lighting will, in general, appear
more nonuniform and the shadows darker in the
picture than in the original scene. This is purely a
visual effect having nothing to do with the
photographic process as such.   *Ralph Evans*

...perception involves going beyond the immediately given evidence of the senses: this
evidence is assessed on many grounds and
generally we make the best bet, and see things
more or less correctly. But the senses do not give
us a picture of the world directly; rather they
provide evidence for checking hypotheses about
what lies before us.   *Richard Gregory*

All thinking is sorting, classifying. All perceiving
relates to expectation and therefore comparisons....
It matters little what filing system we adopt. But
without some standards of comparison we cannot
grasp reality.   *E.H. Gombrich*

Compared to many other societies, ours does not
invest tradition with an enormous weight. Even
our most powerful traditions do not generate the
binding force which is common in some other
cultures.   *Edward Hall*

We know that at a certain distance green surfaces

Hermann Helmholtz

appear a little different in hue. We get in the habit of overlooking this difference and learn to identify the altered green of distant meadows and trees with the corresponding colour of nearer objects.

Henry James

You have formed the habit of comparing, of looking for points, of differences and of resemblance, for present and absent advantages, for the virtues that go with certain defects, and the defects that go with certain virtues.

Paul Klee

For with a bit of imagination every complex structure lends itself to comparison with familiar forms in nature.

Henry Thoreau

Most that is first written on any subject is a mere groping after it, mere rubble-stone and foundation. It is only when many observations of different periods have been brought together that he begins to grasp his subject and can make one pertinent and just observation.

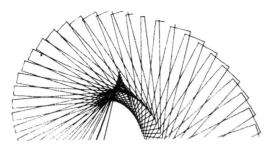

We, not nature, create from the jumble of external
physical phenomena the sounds, scents, colors,
and meanings which make up our emotional and
intellectual lives.   *Rene Dubos*

Nobody, I think, ought to read poetry, or look at
pictures or statues, who cannot find a great deal
more in them than the poet or artist has actually   *Nathaniel*
expressed. Their highest merit is suggestiveness.   *Hawthorne*

It is not unreasonable to say that the environment
is experienced the way it is because one chooses to
see it that way. In this sense the environment is an
artifact created in man's own image.   *William Ittelson*

Far from being a copy of the retinal display, the
visual world is somehow *constructed* on the basis
of information taken in during many different
fixations.   *Ulric Neisser*

If we can realize, from the outset, that our ordinary consciousness is something we must of
necessity construct or *create* in order to survive in
the world, then we can understand that this
consciousness is only *one* possible consciousness.
And if this consciousness is a *personal* construction, then each person can change his consciousness simply by *changing the way* he con-   *Robert Ornstein*
structs it.

Humans Construct

Sometimes I would rather get a transient glimpse
or side view of a thing than stand fronting to it —
as these polypodies. The object I caught a glimpse
of as I went by haunts my thoughts a long time, is
infintely suggestive, and I do not care to front it
and scrutinize it, for I know that the thing that
really concerns me is not there, but in my relation
to that.

Henry Thoreau

So help me find opportunities which offer friends
unclosed photographs which will present them a
chance to close circles out of their roundness.

Minor White

Humans Create

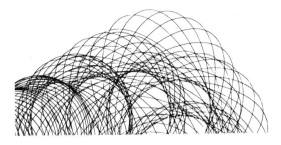

To see the world in a grain of sand
And a heaven in a wild flower,
Hold infinity in the palm of your hand
And eternity in an hour.

William Blake

Modern physics has confirmed most dramatically
one of the basic ideas of Eastern mysticism; that
all the concepts we use to describe nature are
limited, that they are not features of reality, as we
tend to believe, but creations of the mind; parts of
the map, not the territory.

Fritjof Capra

In the case of a creative mind, it seems to me, the
intellect has withdrawn its watchers from the
gates, and the ideas rush in pell-mell, and only
then does it review and inspect the multitude.

Sigmund Freud

The Biblical story of the creation is an excellent
parable of movement. The work of art, too, is
above all a process of creation, it is never experienced as a mere product.

Paul Klee

The capacity to regress, more or less at will, to the
games of the underground, without losing contact
with the surface, seems to be the essence of the
poetic, or any other form of creativity.

Arthur Koestler

I learned from her and others like her that a first-
rate soup is more creative than a second-rate

Abraham Maslow

painting, and that, generally, cooking or parent-hood or making a home could be creative while poetry need not be; it could be uncreative...From a young athlete, I learned that a perfect tackle could be as esthetic a product as a sonnet and could be approached in the same creative spirit.

Rollo May

The artist presents the broken image of man but transcends it in the very act of transmuting it into art. It is his creative act which gives meaning to the nihilism, alienation, and other elements of modern man's condition. To quote Merleau-Ponty again when he writes of Cezanne's schizoid temperament, "Thus the illness ceases to be an absurd fact and a fate, and becomes a general possibility of human existence."

Ben Shahn

The subconscious may greatly shape one's art; undoubtedly it does so. But the subconscious cannot create art.

Thomas Wolfe

I live in my own world: I go about looking, seeing, studying, observing, but the world I create is my own.

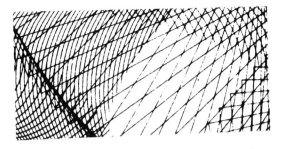

The word is not the perception; it merely stands for the perception and omits much of what is perceived.

Barbara Bullock-Wilson

The act of bringing memory traces to the surface is just as important an activity as the storage of information. The past affects the fate of the organism not because it has been stored, but because many stimuli bring about its retrieval and thus condition all physiological and behavioral responses.

Rene Dubos

The easier it is to separate the code from the content, the more we can rely on the image to communicate a particular kind of information. A selective code that is understood to be a code enables the maker of the image to filter out certain kinds of information and to encode only those features that are of interest to the recipient. Hence a selective representation that indicates its own principles of selection will be more informative than the replica. Anatomical drawings are a case in point.

E.H. Gombrich

What the eyes do is to feed the brain with information coded into neural activity — chains of electrical impulses — which by their code and patterns of brain activity, represent objects.

Richard Gregory

Humans Encode

The recall of previous stimulation may fail because we do not use words to remember pictures or feelings, and therefore we have difficulty using *Ralph Haber* words to describe the memory later.

Man's ability to plan has been made possible because the eye takes in a larger sweep; it codes vastly more complex data and thus encourages *Edward Hall* thinking in the abstract.

In order to survive in a fluctuating environment, an organism must have some capacity to collect, process and use information. This capacity is greatest in man, so that he is able to learn elaborate coding systems and to organize his social *George Miller* behavior by communicating with his fellow men.

I feel that painting is able to contain whatever one *Ben Shahn* thinks and all that he is.

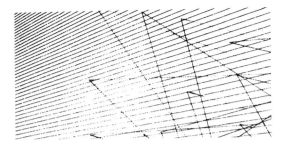

In the past I have used the rather fanciful phrase
that "perception acts sometimes as a welcoming
committee and sometimes as a screening committee." It now appears that both these committees
are closer to the entrance port than previously
conceived.

Jerome Bruner

By using his consciousness to avoid the impact of
many stimuli that stream out of total reality man
certainly simplifies his life and increases his efficiency, but at the cost of much impoverishment.

Rene Dubos

Selective screening of sensory data admits some
things while filtering out others, so that *experience
as it is perceived* through one set of culturally
patterned sensory screens is quite different from
experience perceived through another.

Edward Hall

One of the most extraordinary facts of our life is
that, although we are besieged at every moment
by impressions from our whole sensory surface,
we notice so very small a part of them.

William James

...most individuals do not realize their nervous
systems and brains contain mechanisms which will
defend them against anxiety-producing information
by simply helping them not to perceive consciously
the information. In other words, humans can
easily — and perhaps they must in order to adjust

Humans Filter

Wilson Bryan Key

and survive — shut out from their conscious awarness any information which might deeply trouble or shock them.

D.H. Lawrence

...So much depends on one's attitude. One can shut many, many doors of receptivity in oneself; or one can open many doors that are shut.

Robert Ornstein

The ability to "mirror," to be free of the normal restriction — of the tuning, biasing, and filtering processes of consciousness — may be a part of what is meant by "direct" perception.

Jean Piaget

...actual vision constitutes a sort of sampling, as though only certain points of the perceived figure were fixated while others were neglected.

George Bernard Shaw

You cannot believe in honor until you have achieved it. Better keep yourself clean and bright: you are the window through which you must see the world.

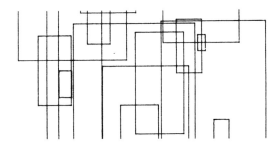

It is not simply society that patterns itself on the
idealizing myths, but unconsciously it is the individual man as well who is able to bring order to
his internal clamor of identities in terms of
prevailing myth. Life, then, produces myth and
finally imitates it.   *Jerome Bruner*

From about 1948 to 1950, Bullock photographed
through Weston's eyes. He had seen the potency of
establishing direct, sensuous relationships with
things and believed in it for himself. Yet, not only
did he function as Weston functioned, he saw as
Weston saw as well. This was not a deliberate
attempt to imitate but rather part of a natural,
primarily unconscious process of learning through
emulation.   *Barbara Bullock-*
                                        Wilson

If to see more is really to become more, if deeper
vision is really fuller being, then we should look
closely at man in order to increase our capacity to   *Teilhard de*
live.   *Chardin*

We can say with historical certainty that Jesus had
a mother; we can say with psychological con-
fidence that much of what he was reflected her.   *Andrew M. Greeley*

Informal learning is largely a matter of the learner
picking others as models. Sometimes this is done

Humans Imitate

deliberately, but most commonly it occurs out-of-awareness. In most cases the model does not take part in this process except as an object of imitation.

Edward Hall

It is always the leadership of any nation that provides the driving ethos of its people; what they see is what they imitate.

Sidney Harris

Because acting in unison spells equal-status friendship, it can be used by dominant individuals to put subordinates at their ease. A therapist treating a patient can help him to relax by deliberately copying the sick person's body display.

Desmond Morris

As a species we are strongly imitative and it is impossible for a healthy individual to grow up and live in a community without becoming infected with its typical action-patterns. The way we walk and stand, laugh and grimace, are all subject to this influence.

Desmond Morris

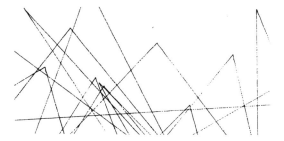

While object-seeing was an important and fundamental way of organizing and relating to the world of stimuli, it represented only a rudimentary level of perception. Casually accepted, words tended to give everything an absolute material reality and limited experience and understanding. In contrast, putting labels aside was an expanding, gratifying process through which he found a new dimension of perceiving...

Barbara Bullock-Wilson

It seems to be a more or less universal human trait to give everything we see a name. Whenever we run into something we assign it to some known class that is familiar to us and proceed to think of it as related to that class. Photographs are no exception in this regard.

Ralph Evans

In the theory of information pickup, the spontaneous activities of looking, listening, and touching, together with the satisfactions of noticing, can proceed with or without language. The curious observer can always observe more properties of the world than he can describe. Observing is thus not necessarily coerced by linguistic labeling, and there is experimental evidence to support this conclusion.

James Gibson

The only things which we commonly see are those which we preperceive, and the only things which

Humans Label

we preperceive are those which have been labelled
for us, and the labels stamped into our mind.

William James

The height of absurdity is reached when man feels
that the objects around him are nameless, and that
only by approaching absurdity will he be able to
find a name, a description and a sign for them.

Paul Klee

Words are essential tools for formulating and
communicating thoughts, and also for putting
them into the storage of memory; but words can
also become snares, decoys, or straight-jackets.

Arthur Koestler

...for the adult, to the extent that we can prevent
ourselves from only abstracting, naming, placing,
comparing, relating, to that extent will we be able
to see more ... Particularly I must underline the
ability to perceive the ineffable, that which cannot
be put into words. Trying to force it into words
changes it, and makes it something other than it is,
something else *like* it, something similar, and yet
something different than *it* itself.

Abraham Maslow

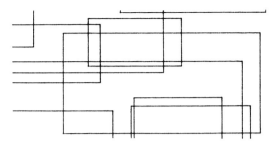

It is in works of art, for example, in paintings, that one can observe how the sense of vision uses its power of organization to the utmost. When an artist chooses a given site for one of his landscapes he not only selects and rearranges what he finds in nature; he must reorganize the whole visible matter to fit an order discovered, invented, purified by him.

Rudolf Arnheim

We perceive in pattern, and we remember in pattern. Only in this way are we able to incorporate our society's way of viewing and testing the universe.

Ray Birdwhistell

Man is the great pattern-maker and pattern-perceiver. No matter how primitive his situation, no matter how tormented, he cannot live in a world of chaos. Everywhere he imposes form.

Edmund Carpenter

I think of myself as a scientist rather than an essayist or philosopher. I feel myself very bound to and by the facts that I am trying to *perceive,* not to create. My creations are structures or organizations of facts. I neither feel free, nor ever *want* in any way, to leave them. I want to describe them and organize and communicate what I see.

Abraham Maslow

The process of organization enables us to package

47

Humans Organize

George Miller

the same total amount of information into far fewer symbols, and so eases the task of remembering.

Harry Stack Sullivan

We organize our acquaintance with the world in order to maintain necessary or pleasant functional activity within the world.

Minor White

It is curious that I always want to group things, a series of sonnets, a series of photographs; whatever rationalizations appear, they originate in urges that are rarely satisfied with single images.

Painting and sculpture cease to be taught as techniques of mechanical reproduction. They are recognized as essential tools for the tasks of finding one's bearings in the world.

Rudolf Arnheim

The more Bullock focused his eyes and mind on nature, the more he felt in harmony with it and the deeper his belief became that man's identity, the meaning of humanness, was to be found in relation to nature and not apart from it.

Barbara Bullock-Wilson

The incomplete image and the unexpected image set the mind a puzzle that makes us linger, enjoy and remember the solution, where the prose of purely informational images would remain unnoticed or unremembered.

E.H. Gombrich

The relationship between man and the cultural dimension is one in which both man and his environment participate in molding each other.

Edward Hall

The aesthetic satisfaction derived from metaphor, imagery, and related techniques...depends on the *emotive potential* of the matrices which enter the game. By emotive potential I mean the capacity of a matrix to generate and satisfy participatory emotions (love, hate, greed, passion, etc.).

Arthur Koestler

Humans Participate

Every person, experiencing as he does his own
solitariness and aloneness, longs for union with
another. He yearns to participate in a relationship
greater than himself. Normally, he strives to
overcome his aloneness through some form of
Rollo May   love.

A person learns significantly only those things
which he perceives as being involved in the
maintenance of, or enhancement of, the structure
Carl Rogers   of self.

All photographs are *memento mori.* To take a
photograph is to participate in another person's (or
Susan Sontag   thing's) mortality, vulnerability, mutability.

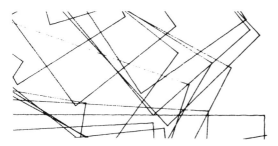

With my inward eye 'tis an old man grey. With
my outward a thistle across the way.

William Blake

You come to know a thing by being inside it. You
get an inside view. You step into the skin of the
beast and that, precisely, is what the masked and
costumed dancer does. He puts on the beast.

Edmund Carpenter

Yea, the fool when he walketh in the way, whereas
he himself is a fool, esteemeth all men fools.

Ecclesiastes

Thus inevitably does the universe wear our color,
and every object fall successively into the subject
itself. The subject exists, the subject enlarges; all
things sooner or later fall into place. As I am, so I
see.

*Ralph Waldo
Emerson*

Perhaps the most effective general technique in the
care and feeding of media audiences is simply to
*tell them what they want to hear or what they
need to hear,* at both the conscious and unconscious levels. Audiences' idealized views of
both themselves and what they wish the world
were like are projected through the mirror of
media. The reflections absorbed by the reader
projects back to him his own idealized self-image.

Wilson Bryan Key

I am a mirror, and who looks at me, whatever
good or bad he speaks, he speaks of himself.

Omar Khayyam

Humans Project

How gibbering man becomes, when he is really clever, and thinks he is giving the ultimate and final description of the universe! Can't he see that he is merely describing himself...? ...We describe the universe as we find it.... Is our description true? Not for a single moment, once you change your state of mind; or your state of soul.

D.H. Lawrence

When I looked at *things for what they are* I was fool enough to persist in my folly and found that each photograph was a mirror of my Self.

Minor White

Search thine own heart. What
     paineth thee
In others in thyself may be.

John Whittier

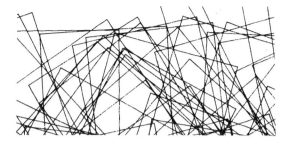

Memory images serve to identify, interpret, and
supplement perception. No neat borderline
separates a purely perceptual image — if such
there is — from one completed by memory or one
not directly perceived at all but supplied entirely
from memory residues.   *Rudolf Arnheim*

The response of any given person to an environmental factor is conditioned both
physiologically and psychologically by his own
past experiences; it is therefore highly personal.   *Rene Dubos*

Viewing of color in a particular situation is, at
best, a peculiar mixture of attention, intention and
memory.   *Ralph Evans*

...reading an image, like the reception of any other
message, is dependent on prior knowledge of
possibilities; we can only recognize what we know.   *E.H. Gombrich*

Visual perception is as much concerned with
remembering what we have seen as with the act of
seeing itself. When I look at a picture, I am aware
that I am seeing it, and I can describe the experience of seeing. I can also remember what I saw
after the picture is no longer there.   *Ralph Haber*

Ah! what pleasant visions haunt me
  As I gaze upon the sea!

Humans Remember

Henry Wadsworth
Longfellow

All the old romantic legends,
All my dreams, come back to me.

Thomas Merton

Everything I see and experience in Kentucky is to some extent colored and shaped by the thoughts and emotions I had when I first came to the monastery. It cannot be otherwise.

Ulric Neisser

Visual memory differs from perception because it is based primarily on stored rather than on current information, but it involves the same kind of synthesis. Although the eyes have been called the windows of the soul, they are not so much peepholes as entry ports, supplying raw material for the constructive activitiy of the visual system.

Percy Bysshe
Shelley

Music, when soft voices die,
Vibrates in the memory,
Odours, when sweet violets sicken,
Live within the sense they quicken.

William
Wordsworth

Minds that have nothing to confer
Find little to perceive.

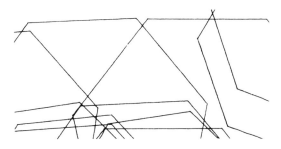

Complete receptivity is the prerogative of
childhood and of the few privileged adults who
have retained or recaptured the directness of
perception which enables most children to see
"things as they are."

Rene Dubos

The eye is not filled with seeing, neither is the ear
filled with hearing.

Ecclesiastes

Animals and men can select or enhance the stimuli
they receive from the world, or even exclude
certain kinds, by orienting and adjusting their
sense organs.

James Gibson

What we observe is not nature itself, but nature
exposed to our method of questioning.

*Werner
Heisenberg*

The study of works of art will throw great light on
the question as to which elements and relations of
our visual impressions are most predominant in
determining our conception of what is seen, and
what others are of less importance. As far as lies
within his power, the artist will seek to foster the
former at the cost of the latter.

*Hermann
Helmholtz*

The artist notoriously selects his items, rejecting
all tones, colors, shapes, which do not harmonize
with each other and with the main purpose of his
work.

William James

Humans Select

The thing represented had to pass through two
distorting lenses: the artist's mind, and his medium
of expression, before it emerged as a man-made
dream — the two, of course, being intimately
connected and interacting with each other.

Arthur Koestler

Many an object is not seen, though it falls within
the range of our visual ray, because it does not
come within the range of our intellectual ray, i.e.,
we are not looking for it. So, in the largest sense,
we find only the world we look for.

Henry Thoreau

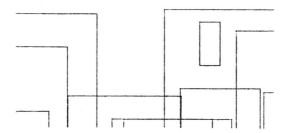

To arrive at what is simple is a difficult process.	*Rasheed bin Fouad*
Any stimulus pattern tends to be seen in such a way that the resulting structure is as simple as the given conditions permit.	*Rudolf Arnheim*
Every real work of art is already a simplification and interpretation. To simplify it yet further and to interpret it more penetratingly or subtly, may reduce it to a concept.	*Bernard Berenson*
...remembered shapes tend toward simplified forms just as do the original perceptions. Long ovals and rectangles tend to become longer ones, short ovals tend toward circles and short rectangles toward squares.	*Ralph Evans*
For in art everything is best said once and in the simplest way.	*Paul Klee*
...when physical systems or human perceptions are given time and other opportunities to do so, they change in the direction of greater simplicity or regularity.	*Wolfgang Kohler*

It seems to me that the very fact of our limited capacity for processing information has made it necessary for us to discover clever ways to ab-

George Miller

stract the essential features of our universe and to express these features in simple laws that we are capable of comprehending in a single act of thought.

Floyd Ratliff

...the eye appears to act according to the principle of least effort and to do no more than is imposed upon it — either by the other eye or by the central nervous system. Using this principle it could also be directly explained why, with predilection, we see a straight retinal image as a straight line in space. The eye develops a minimum of depth sensation differences.

John Ruskin

The greatest thing a human soul ever does in this world is to *see* something, and tell what it *saw* in a plain way... To see clearly is poetry, prophecy, and religion, all in one.

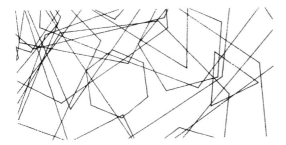

Man does not deal directly with nature; nature is a symbolic construct, a creature of man's powers to represent experience through powerful abstractions.

Jerome Bruner

Just as the symbolic language which we find in dreams and in myths is a particular form of expressing thoughts and feelings by images of sensory experience, the ritual is a symbolic expression of thoughts and feelings by *action*.

Erich Fromm

Michelangelo's famous statue of Night, with her symbolic attributes of the star, the owl and the sleep-inducing poppies, is not only a pictograph of a concept but also a poetic evocation of nocturnal feelings.

E.H. Gombrich

Perhaps the most important implication of the Mary symbol is its unreserved, unabashed hopefulness. ...If you beleive there is a power in the universe that is superbly reflected in the grace, the playfulness, of an attractive and lovable young woman, then you do not despair no matter how overwhelming your problems and humankind's might appear.

Andrew Greely

Because there are innumberable things beyond the range of human understanding, we constantly use symbolic terms to represent concepts that we

Carl Jung

cannot define or fully comprehend. This is one reason why all religions employ symbolic language or images.

D.H. Lawrence

And the images of myth are symbols. They don't "mean something." They stand for units of human *feeling,* human experience ... Many ages of accumulated experience still throb within a symbol. And we throb in response ... And again, when men become unresponsive and half dead, symbols die.

Rollo May

We forget at our peril that man is a symbol-making creature; and if the symbols (or myths, which are a pattern of symbols) seem arid and dead, they are to be mourned rather than denied. The bankruptcy of symbols should be seen for what it is, a way station on the path of despair.

Ben Shahn

...to the psychologist, Oedipus is a symbol of aberration only — a medical symbol. But to the artist Oedipus is a symbol of moral anguish, and even more than that, of transcendent spiritual power.

Harry Stack Sullivan

The child thus learns some of the more complicated implications of a symbol in contradistinction to the actuality to which the symbol refers, which is its referent; in other words, the distinction between the symbol and that which is symbolized.

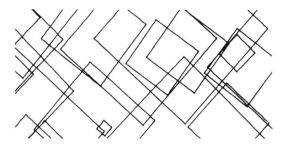

Drawings, paintings, and other similar devices
serve not simply to translate finished thoughts into
visible models but are also an aid in the process of
working out solutions of problems.   *Rudolf Arnheim*

Phonetic writing translated, into one sense only,
the multi-sensuous thing that is spoken language.
The peculiar effect of translating the many senses
of the spoken word into the visual mode of writing
was to abstract one sense from the cluster of the
human senses.   *Edmund Carpenter*

Most painters know that they are dealing with
relative degrees of abstraction; whatever they do
depends on vision and must be translated into
other senses.   *Edward Hall*

A person whose visual imagination is strong finds
it hard to understand how those who are without
the faculty can think at all. Some people undoubtedly have no visual images at all worthy of
the name and instead of seeing their breakfast-
table, they tell you that they *remember* it or *know*
what was on it.   *William James*

Both artist and neurotic speak and live from the
subconscious and unconscious depths of their
society. The artist does this positively, communicating what he experiences to his fellow men.

Humans Translate

Rollo May

The neurotic does this negatively. Experiencing the same underlying meanings and contradictions of his culture, he is unable to form his experiences into communicable meaning for himself and his fellows.

George Miller

We are constantly taking information given in one form and translating it into alternative forms, searching for ways to map a strange, new phenomenon into simpler and more familiar ones.

Richard Wagner

I at once recognized that the orchestral overture to the "Rheingold," which must long have lain latent within me, though it had been unable to find definite form, had at last been revealed to me. I then quickly realized my own nature; the stream of life was not to flow to me from without, but from within. I decided to return to Zurich immediately, and begin the composition of my great work.

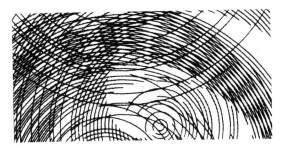

Observe constantly that all things take place by change, and accustom thyself to consider that the nature of the Universe loves nothing so much as to change the things which are to make new things like them. For everything that exists is in a manner the seed of that which will be.

Marcus Aurelius

Heraclitus would have it that we cannot dip twice into the same stream. What is there that we can exactly repeat, seeing that neither within or without are we and our universe the same for two consecutive seconds? Still, less can we enjoy or appreciate or understand anything the same way twice.

Bernard Berenson

The more Bullock explored the phenomenon of change, the more it amazed and fascinated him. On one level, it seemed to him to be the basic, underlying process of the universe. It linked all things — organic and inorganic, material and process — into an interrelated, dynamic, evolving network of life.

Barbara Bullock-Wilson

It was when everything was covered with snow that I perceived that the doors and windows were blue.

Albert Camus

Familiarity may be carried to a point where the familiar element no longer attracts the mind. It is a

Perception Is Influenced By Change

John Dewey

matter of common observation that the continued ticking of a clock ceases to come in consciousness, while change, such as its stopping, is immediately noticed.

Heraclitus

You cannot step in the same river twice.

William James

Another well-known change is when we look at a landscape with our head upside-down. Perception is to a certain extent baffled by this manoeuver; gradations of distance and other space-determinations are made uncertain; the reproductive or associative processes, in short, decline; and, simultaneously with their diminution, the colors grow richer and more varied, and the contrasts of light and shade more marked.

Paul Klee

Cheer up! Value such country outings, which let you have a new point of view for once as well as a change of air, and transport you to a world which, by diverting you, strengthens you for the inevitable return to the grayness of the working day.

Henry Thoreau

Not only different objects are presented to our attention at different seasons of the year, but we are in a frame of body and of mind to appreciate different objects at different seasons. I see one thing when it is cold and another when it is warm.

Perception Is Influenced By Contrast

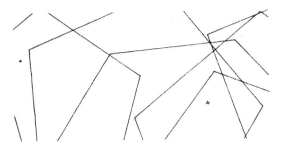

Order and complexity are antagonistic, in that
order tends to reduce complexity while complexity
tends to reduce order...Order and complexity,
however, cannot exist without each other.
Complexity without order produces confusion;
order without complexity produces boredom.

Rudolf Arnheim

Without contraries there is no progression.

William Blake

Most tribal art is hard-edge art. It's art of sharp
contrasts, sudden juxtapositions and super-
impositions. So is children's art. It favors the
strongly marked boundary lines of the icon.
Gradation and continuity are shunned.

Edmund Carpenter

...the apparent colour and brightness of
illuminated objects varies with the colour and
brightness of the illumination. This is a fact of the
first importance for the painter, for many of his
finest effects depend on it.

*Hermann
Helmholtz*

The sad truth is that man's real life consists of a
complex of inexorable opposites — day and night,
birth and death, happiness and misery, good and
evil. We are not sure that one will prevail against
the other, that good will overcome evil, or joy
defeat pain. Life is a battleground. It always will
be; if it were not so, existence would come to an
end.

Carl Jung

Perception Is Influenced By Contrast

Robert Ornstein

We quickly adapt to the constancies of the world; hence we constantly need new stimulation.

Ben Shahn

Contrasts in life move constantly across the field of vision — tensions between the grotesque and the sad, between the contemptible and the much-loved; tensions of such special character as to be almost imperceptible; dramatic, emotional situations within the most banal settings. Only the detached eye is able to perceive these properties and qualities of things.

Susan Sontag

The authority of Arbus's photographs derives from the contrast between their lacerating subject matter and their calm, matter-of-fact attentiveness.

Each new environment makes the old one visible:
what is psychic becomes explicit only after it
becomes obsolete. The present environment is
never seen. We respect its laws without being
conscious of them. We are conscious only of the
obsolete and we value it because it appears
manageable, subject to conscious control. This
makes it splendidly attractive.   *Edmund Carpenter*

We shape our buildings, and afterwards our
buildings shape us.   *Winston Churchill*

The conceptual environment of primitive man
commonly affects his life more profoundly than his
external environment. And this is also true of
modern man.   *Rene Dubos*

As between the soul and the body there is a bond,
so are the body and its environment linked
together.   *Kahlil Gibran*

The environment consists of *opportunities* for
perception, of *available* information, of *potential*
stimuli. Not all opportunities are grasped, not all
information is registered, not all stimuli excite
receptors. But what the environment *affords* an
individual in the way of discrimination is enor-
mous, and this should be our first consideration. *James Gibson*

Perception Is Influenced By Environment

Gertrud Grunow

All living things and all beings outside of man are complementary to him; on the other hand, man transfers his perceptions and experiences into his environment and thus sees and forms the world.

William Ittelson

...the individual cannot be separated from the environment. He is part of the system he is perceiving, and the strategies he chooses become the environment he in turn experiences as being external to himself.

Jean Piaget

The human being is immersed right from birth in a social environment which affects him just as much as his physical environment. Society, even more, in a sense, than the physical environment, changes the very structure of the individual, because it not only compels him to recognize facts, but also provides him with a ready-made system of signs, which modify his thought; it presents him with new values and it imposes on him an infinite series of obligations.

Ben Shahn

I have always believed that the character of a society is largely shaped and unified by its great creative works, that a society is molded upon its epics, and that it imagines in terms of its created things — its cathedrals, its works of art, its musical treasures, its literary and philosophic works.

Susan Sontag

Photographs are perhaps the most mysterious of all objects that make up, and thicken, the environment we recognize as modern.

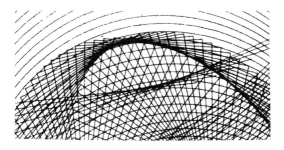

The organism in perception is in one way or
another in a state of expectancy about the environment. It is a truism worth repeating that the
perceptual effect of a stimulus is necessarily
dependent upon the set or expectancy of the
organism. And so, in many situations the student
of perception must also specify the expectancies of
the organism when exposed to stimulation.   *Jerome Bruner*

The body responds not only to the stimulus itself,
but also to all the symbols associated with the
memories of the past, the experiences of the
present, and the anticipations of the future.
Anything that impinges on man thus affects both
his mind and his body and causes them to interact
— an inescapable consequence of the evolutionary
and experimental past.   *Rene Dubos*

No one has ever been able to say exactly where
perceiving ceases and remembering begins, either
by introspection or by observation of behavior.
Similarly, it is not possible to separate perceiving
from expecting by an line of demarcation. In-
trospectively, the "conscious present," as James
observed, merges with both the past and the
future.   *James Gibson*

A world in which all our expectations were
constantly belied would be a lethal world.   *E.H. Gombrich*

Perception Is Influenced By Expectancy

Hermann Helmholtz

For, equipped with an awareness of the physical form of an object, we can clearly imagine all of the perspective images which we may expect upon viewing from this or that side, and we are immediately disturbed when such an image does not correspond to our expectations. This may happen, for instance, when a change in the physical form of an object occurs with a change in its position.

Heraclitus

If you do not expect it, you will not find the unexpected, for it is hard to find and difficult.

William James

We must form as clear a notion as possible of what we expect to see. Then it will actually appear.

Arthur Schopenhauer

Humor overthrows logical expectation, and therein lies its appeal.

Perception Is Influenced By Experience

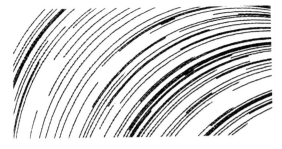

The child is father to the man in a manner that may be irreversibly one-directional, for to make up for a bland impoverishment of experience early in life may be too great an obstacle for most organisms.

Jerome Bruner

The national differences in perception of space during interpersonal encounters are not racially determined; they are expressions of social influences rooted in history and experienced during early life. These influences affect also the perception of other aspects of the environment.

Rene Dubos

The environment provides an inexhaustible reservoir of information. Some men spend most of their lives looking, others listening, and a few connoisseurs spend their time in smelling, tasting, or touching. They never come to an end. The eyes and ears are not fixed capacity instruments, like cameras and microphones, with which the brain can see and hear. Looking and listening continue to improve with experience.

James Gibson

What a picture means to the viewer is strongly dependent on his past experience and knowledge. In this respect the visual image is not a mere representation of "reality" but a symbolic system.

E.H. Gombrich

The image in the mind *is* the attention; the

Perception Is Influenced By Experience

preperception is half of the perception of the
looked-for thing. It is for this reason that men
have no eyes but for those aspects of things which
William James   they have already been taught to discern.

The "innocent eye" is a fiction, based on the
absurd notion that what we perceive in the present
can be isolated in the mind from the influence of
past experience. There is no perception of "pure
form" but meaning seeps in, and settles on the
Arthur Koestler   image.

The way to recover the meaning of life and the
worthwhileness of life is to recover the power to
experience, to have impulse voices from within
and to be able to hear these impulse voices from
Abraham Maslow   within — and make the point: This can be done.

By experiencing something, we let its meaning
permeate through us on all levels: feeling, acting,
thinking, and, ultimately, deciding, since decision
is the act of putting one's total self on the line. The
passion for experience is an endeavor to include
more of the self in the picture; one experiences as a
Rollo May   totality.

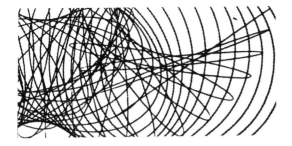

Ideally, man should remain receptive to new stimuli and new situations in order to continue to develop. In practice, however, the ability to perceive the external world with freshness decreases as the senses and the mind are increasingly conditioned in the course of life.

Rene Dubos

The appeal of fraternal organizations, like the preoccupation with proper behavior expressed in etiquette books, gives convincing proof of modern man's need for ritual and of the emptiness of those he performs.

Erich Fromm

The familiar will always remain the likely starting point for the rendering of the unfamiliar; an existing representation will always exert its spell over the artist even while he strives to record the truth.

E.H. Gombrich

Another general characteristic property of our sense-perceptions is, that *we are not in the habit of observing our sensations accurately, except as they are useful in enabling us to recognize external objects. On the contrary, we are wont to disregard all those parts of the sensations that are of no importance so far as external objects are concerned.* Thus in most cases some special assistance and training are needed in order to observe these latter subjective sensations.

Hermann Helmholtz

Perception Is Influenced By Habit

William James

Habit diminishes the conscious attention with which our acts are performed.

Joseph Kerwin
(Skylab Astronaut)

It turns out that you carry with you your own body-oriented world, independent of anything else, in which *up* is over your head, *down* is below your feet, *right* is this way and *left* is that way; and you take this world around with you wherever you go.

Robert Ornstein

When we see a new image, our eyes tend to move in a new pattern around it, but as we see it again and again, as we see the rooms in our house, we tend to look in a fixed way at fixed portions of it and ignore or tune out the rest.

Henry Thoreau

I have the habit of attention to such excess that my senses get no rest, but suffer from a constant strain. Be not preoccupied with looking. Go not to the object; let it come to you. When I have found myself ever looking down and confining my gaze to the flowers, I have thought it might be well to get into the habit of observing the clouds as a corrective; but no! that study would be just as bad. What I need is not to look at all, but a true sauntering of the eye.

Perception Is Influenced By Language

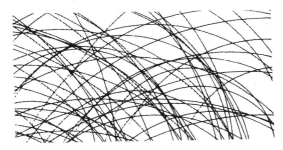

Language is required to mediate pictorial
representation, at least initially. The child will not
see one thing as standing for another — and that is
the essence of representation — without the verbal
link. Language is the most flexible system of
representation that has been evolved. It predates
pictorial representation by several millennia in
human evolution.

T.G.R. Bower

Language comes infinitely short of paralleling the
variegated surface of nature. Yet words as prac-
tical devices are the agencies by which the ineffable diversity of natural existence as it operates in
human experience is reduced to orders, ranks, and
classes that can be managed.

John Dewey

The essence of symbolic language is that inner
experiences, one of thought and feeling, are expressed as if they were sensory experiences. All of
us "speak" this language if only when we are
asleep. Yet the language of dreams is not different
from that which is employed in myths and
religious thinking. Symbolic language is the only
universal language the human race has known.

Erich Fromm

...the learning of language by the child is not
simply the associative naming or labeling of
impressions from the world. It is also, and more
importantly, an expression of the distinctions,

Perception Is Influenced By Language

James Gibson

abstractions, and recognitions that the child is coming to achieve in perceiving.

Ralph Haber

Although a person may remember almost any picture he has ever seen, he frequently is unable to recall details from a specific image when asked to do so.

Hermann Helmholtz

...a highly developed language of a civilized nation is such a richly developed means of expression of the most multifarious and delicate shadings of thought that it could very well be compared in this respect with the wealth of physical forms of nature's handiwork around us.

Henry James

Each word means something slightly different to each person, even among those who share the same cultural background.

Arthur Koestler

Language can become a screen which stands between the thinker and reality. This is the reason why true creativity often starts where language ends.

Edward Sapir

It is quite an illusion to imagine that one adjusts to reality essentially without the use of language and that language is merely an incidental means of solving specific problems of communication or reflection. The fact of the matter is that the "real world" is to a large extent built up on the language habit of the group.

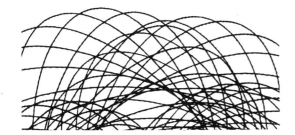

Metaphor joins dissimilar experiences by finding
the image or the symbol that unites them at some
deeper emotional level of meaning.   *Jerome Bruner*

Art has been the means of keeping alive the sense
of purposes that outrun evidence and of meanings
that transcend indurated habit.   *John Dewey*

What man actually needs is not a tensionless state
but rather the striving and struggling for some
goal worthy of him. What he needs is not the
discharge of tension at any cost, but the call of a
potential meaning waiting to be fulfilled by him.   *Viktor Frankl*

Man positively needs general ideas and convictions
that will give meaning to his life and enable him to
find a place for himself in the universe. He can
stand the most incredible hardships when he is
convinced that they make sense....   *Carl Jung*

The unconscious perpetually flows into man's
consciousness through visions, dreams, fantasies,
and myths — providing a base of meaning from
which to consciously interpret the world of reality. *Wilson Bryan Key*

The mind is insatiable for meaning, drawn from,
or projected into, the world of appearances, for
unearthing hidden analogies which connect the
unknown with the familiar, and show the familiar

Perception Is Influenced By Meaning

Arthur Koestler   in an unexpected light.

Practically all the activities that man prides himself on, and that give meaning, richness, and value to his life, are either omitted or pathologized by Freud. Work, play, love, art, creativeness, religion in the good sense, ethics, philosophy, science, learning, parenthood, self-sacrifice, heroism, saintliness, goodness — these are all weakly
Abraham Maslow   handled, if at all.

Art is a substitute for violence. The same impulses that drive some persons to violence — the hunger for meaning, the need for ecstasy, the impulse to risk all — drive the artist to create. He is by
Rollo May   nature our archrebel.

Perception Is Influenced By Movement

Change is absent in immobile things but also in things repeating the same action over and over or persevering in it steadfastly...A color looked at steadily tends to bleach, and if the eye is made to fixate a pattern without the small scanning movements that are never absent otherwise, that pattern will disappear from sight after a short while.

Rudolf Arnheim

In America, there exist body motion areas with locally special variations of movement as distinctive as the variations to be heard in the varied speech communities.

Ray Birdwhistell

In man, the ability to control the movements of the hand by vision has led to picture-making and even to ideographic or phonetic writing, from which a new level of cognition emerges.

James Gibson

...the impression of movement, and thereby of life, is so much more easily obtained with a few energetic strokes than through elaboration of detail.

E.H. Gombrich

Since the perceiver is rarely if ever completely motionless himself, the retinal projection of stimulation from the visual environment will be constantly shifting, changing, stretching, and transforming.

Ralph Haber

Perception Is Influenced By Movement

Hermann Helmholtz

With unfamiliar positions and movements of our sensory organs correspondingly unusual perceptions come about for which we have no trained knowledge of meaning.

Paul Klee

The beholder's eye, which moves about like an animal grazing, follows paths prepared for it in the picture...The pictorial work was born of movement, is itself recorded movement, and is assimilated through movement (eye muscles).

Ulric Neisser

If an analogy between eye and camera were valid, the things one looked at would have to hold still like a photographer's model in order to be seen clearly. The opposite is true: far from obscuring the shapes and spatial relations of things, movement generally clarifies them.

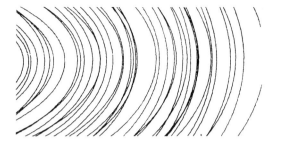

In physical as well as in psychological or social matters, the constant aspects of a situation are most easily overlooked, hardest to be understood.

Rudolf Arnheim

It is the new, the unfamiliar, that attracts notice, and that is especially emphasized in consciousness...A shock of surprise is one of the most effectual methods of arousing attention. The unexpected in the midst of routine is the accentuated.

John Dewey

In the course of our lives we have all accumulated a large number of expectations about what things go together and what things do not. When such an expectation is not fulfilled, dissonance occurs.

Leon Festinger

It is a familiar experience that the colours of a landscape come out much more brilliantly and definitely by looking at them with the head on one side or upside down than they do when the head is in the ordinary upright position.

Hermann Helmholtz

In very general terms, one fundamental feature of perceiving is that it is relevant or appropriate to the situation in which is occurs.

William Ittelson

Artists can predict how most viewers' eyes will move; the fovea image jumps toward anything novel or emotionally stimulating. In viewing

Wilson Bryan Key

commercial art, there would be great similarity in the fovea paths followed by most individuals as they scan the advertisement.

If I wished to see a mountain or other scenery under the most favorable auspices, I would go to it in foul weather, so as to be there when it cleared up; we are then in the most suitable mood, and nature is most fresh and inspiring. There is no serenity so fair as that which is just established in a tearful eye.

Henry Thoreau

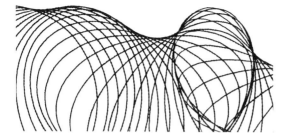

Our aim...is to show the interdependence of the
dynamics of personality and the dynamics of
perceiving. A theory of personality...cannot be
complete without a complementary theory of
perception, and, by the same logic, one cannot
account for the full range of perceptual phenomena
without broadening perceptual theory to a point
where it contains personality variables.   *Jerome Bruner*

A thought may be an empty shell, nothing but an
opinion held because it is the thought pattern of
the culture which one adopts easily and could shed
easily provided public opinion changes. A thought,
on the other hand, may be the expression of the
person's feelings and genuine convictions. In the
latter case it is rooted in his total personality and
has an *emotional matrix*. Only those thoughts
which are thus rooted determine effectively the
person's action.   *Erich Fromm*

The productions of artists and writers represent
rich, unmined beds of hard data on how man
perceives.   *Edward Hall*

You cannot play with the animal in you without
becoming wholly animal, play with falsehood
without forfeiting your right to truth, play with
cruelty without losing your sensitivity of mind. He

Perception Is Influenced By Personality

Dag Hammarskjold   who wants to keep his garden tidy doesn't reserve a plot for weeds.

Hermann Helmholtz   We must look upon artists as persons whose observations of sensuous impressions are particularly vivid and accurate, and whose memory for these images is particularly true.

Carl Jung   One can...make a relatively simple distinction between individuals who have "extroverted" personalities and others who are "introverted." This is only one of many possible generalizations, but it enables one to see immediately the difficulties that can arise if the analyst should happen to be one type and his patient the other.

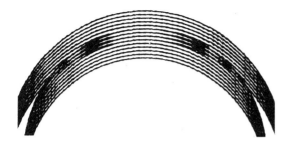

...for as long as possible and by whatever means available, the organism will ward off the perception of the unexpected, those things which do not fit his prevailing set...most people come to depend upon a certain constancy in their environment and, save under special conditions, attempt to ward off variations from this state of affairs: "Thar ain't no such animal," the hayseed is reputed to have said on seeing his first giraffe.

Jerome Bruner

It is generally known that one of the greatest difficulties in drawing is to eliminate the influence which knowledge of the true size of seen objects automatically exerts.

Hermann Helmholtz

Sets are thought to be maintained by inhibitory mechanisms involved with human consciousness. This inhibitory process may be fundamental to the human's concept of reality. Another way of expressing the paradox is, *a way of seeing is also a way of not seeing.* Ways of coping with "right" or "wrong" concepts within a culture or society are established through the use of sets.

Wilson Bryan Key

Primary processes: how best to release them? Don't try, strain. Don't be eager. Be interested to see what idea develops. Not too goal-oriented (then your eye is on the goal, not on the matter in hand). Become unmotivated. Not too reality-

Perception Is Influenced By Set

Abraham Maslow   oriented. Close out the world. Loaf, laze, enjoy.

Louis Pasteur
In the fields of observation, chance favors only the prepared mind.

Ben Shahn
The representative element in a work of art may or may not be harmful, but it is always irrelevant. For to appreciate a work of art, we must bring with us nothing from life, no knowledge of its affairs and ideas, no familiarity with its emotions.

Henry Thoreau
I must walk more with free senses. It is as bad to study stars and clouds as flowers and stones. I must let my senses wander as my thoughts, my eyes without looking. Carlyle said that how to observe was to look, but I say that it is rather to see, and the more you look the less you will observe.

The world emerging from this perceptual exploration is not immediately given. Some of its aspects build up fast, some slowly, and all of them are subject to continued confirmation, reappraisal, change, completion, correction, deepening of understanding.

Rudolf Arnheim

Time does not go fast when one observes it. It feels watched. But it takes advantage of our distractions. Perhaps there are even two times, the one we observe and the one that transforms us.

Albert Camus

Time and reflection change the sight little by little till we come to understand.

Cezanne

Man's physiological and behavioral responses to any situation are different in the morning from what they are at night, and different in the spring from what they are in the autumn.

Rene Dubos

...even the great visionary thinker never completely escapes his own age or the limitations it imposes upon him.

Loren Eisley

In Hopi, there is no word which is equivalent to "time" in English. Because both time and space are inextricably bound up in each other, elimination of time dimension alters the spatial one as well.

Edward Hall

Perception Is Influenced By Time

William James

The same space of time seems shorter as we grow older — that is, the days, the months, and the years do so; whether the hours do so is doubtful, and the minutes and seconds to all appearances remain the same.

Carl Jung

Images that seem contradictory and ridiculous crowd in on the dreamer, the normal sense of time is lost, and commonplace things can assume a fascinating or threatening aspect.

Paul Klee

When a dot begins to move and becomes a line, this requires time. Likewise, when a moving line produces a plane, and when moving planes produces spaces. Does a pictorial work come into being at one stroke? No, it is constructed bit by bit, just like a house.

Wolfgang Kohler

After a while it became obvious not only that any visual pattern or object is gradually altered when inspected for some time, but also that the change follows certain definite rules.

Minor White

Often while traveling with camera we arrive just as the sun slips over the horizon of a moment, too late to expose film, only time enough to expose our hearts.

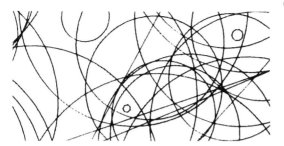

The word archetype refers to an original model or prototype after which other similar things are patterned. In Jungian terms it refers to emotionally charged universal thought patterns such as mother, rebirth, spirit, trickster, hero and wise old man. Images of these archetypes can be patterned in many ways and have a strong influence on our perceptions and behavior.

Rasheed bin Fouad

As we become familiar with more and more objects of art, we discover certain similarities between images which are thousands of years and miles apart. One way to explain these similarities is to...surmise that the twentieth-century artist is prey to unconscious forces which are not dissimilar to those affecting his prehistoric colleague.

Graham Collier

The myths of ancient peoples are still meaningful to us because they express preoccupations and moods which are universal and eternal.

Rene Dubos

Black things, and especially *dark places,* holes, caverns, etc., arouse a peculiarly gruesome fear. This fear as well as that of being "lost," are explained after a fashion by ancestral experience.

Williams James

What we properly call instincts are physiological urges, and are perceived by the senses. But at the same time, they also manifest themselves in

Carl Jung

fantasies and often reveal their presence only by symbolic images. These manifestations are what I call the archetypes.

Carl Jung

Like any other archetype, the mother archetype appears under an almost infinite variety of aspects...personal mother and grandmother...a nurse or governess...Mother of God...Church, university...earth, the woods, the sea or any still waters...the moon, can be mother-symbols. The archetype is often associated with things and places standing for fertility and fruitfulness: the cornucopia, a ploughed field, a garden.

Wilson Bryan Key

Archetypes have also been described as "all-embracing parables," with only partially accessible meanings. They, in any respect, are a type of symbol with a much more profound and deeper meaning and significance to human behavior.

Wilson Bryan Key

Archetypal symbolism, specifically, refers to symbols that have appeared in many places, at many times, with an inexplicable similarity of meaning. These archetypes are found in religious rituals, folklore, fairy tales, mythologies, and in dreams.

Arthur Koestler

One need not be a follower of Jung to recognize the same archetypal experiences crystallized into symbols in the mythologies of cultures widely separate in space and time.

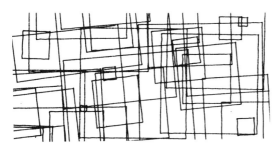

In the end, works of art are the only media of
complete and unhindered communication between
man and man that can occur in a world full of
gulfs and walls that limit community of experience.

John Dewey

Ah, how often great art comes to me in sleep, the
same does not occur when I'm awake. When I'm
awake, my memory loses it.

Albrecht Durer

Art is a conventionally accepted reality in which,
thanks to artistic illusion, symbols and substitutes
are able to provoke real emotion. Thus art constitutes a region half-way between a reality which
frustrates wishes and the wishfulfilling world of
the imagination — a region in which, as it were,
primitive man's strivings for omnipotence are still
in full force.

Sigmund Freud

The essence of a work of art is not to be found in
the personal idiosyncrasies that creep into it —
indeed, the more there are of them, the less it is a
work of art — but in its rising above the personal
and speaking from the mind and heart of the artist
to the heart and mind of mankind. The personal
aspect of art is a limitation and even a vice. Art
that is only personal, or predominately so,
deserves to be treated as a neurosis.

Carl Jung

Art

Paul Klee

Art does not reproduce the visible; rather, it makes visible.

Norman Mailer

Art obviously depends upon incomplete communication. A work which is altogether explicit is not art, the audience cannot respond with their own creative act of the imagination, that leap of the faculties which leaves one an increment more exceptional than when one began.

Pablo Picasso

Painting isn't an aesthetic operation; it's a form of magic designed as a mediator between this strange, hostile world and us, a way of seizing the power by giving form to our terrors as well as our desires.

John Ruskin

What we want art to do for us is to stay what is fleeting, and to enlighten what is incomprehensible, to incorporate the things that have no measure, and immortalise the things that have no duration...

Victor Shklovsky

The purpose of art is to impart in us the sensation of an object as it is *perceived* and not merely recognized. To accomplish this purpose art uses two techniques: the defamiliarization of things, and the distortion of form so as to make the act of perception more difficult and to prolong its duration.

Leo Tolstoy

Art is a human activity consisting in this, that one man consciously, by means of certain external signs, hands on to others feelings he has lived through, and that other people are infected by these feelings and also experience them.

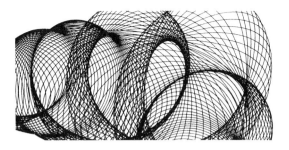

The experience of oneness with the surrounding
environment is the main characteristic of the
meditative state. It is a state of consciousness
where every form of fragmentation has ceased,
fading away into undifferentiated unity.

Fritjof Capra

Art arises when the secret vision of the artist and
the manifestation of nature agree to find new
shapes.

Kahlil Gibran

Colour possesses me. I don't have to pursue it. It
will possess me always, I know it. That is the
meaning of this happy hour; colour and I are one.
I am a painter.

Paul Klee

If we think about it, we find that our life consists
in this achieving of a pure relationship between
ourselves and the living universe about us. This is
how I "save my soul" by accomplishing a pure
relationship between me and another person, me
and other people, me and a nation, me and a race
of men, me and the animals, me and the trees or
flowers, me and the earth, me and the skies and
sun and stars, me and the moon: an infinity of
pure relations, big and little...

D.H. Lawrence

We speak here of the ability to integrate and of the
play back and forth between integration within the
person, and his ability to integrate whatever it is

Confluence

Abraham Maslow

he is doing in the world. To the extent that creativeness is constructive, synthesizing, unifying, and integrative, to that extent does it depend in part on the inner integration of the person.

Rollo May

If we take the time-honored metaphor of the sculptor and his clay, we must see that clay also *forms* the sculptor; the clay conditions what he does, limits and even changes his intentions, and, thus, also forms *his* potentialities and consciousness.

Pope John XXIII

Oh Truth! My God, make me one with thee in eternal love.

Eleanor Roosevelt

She broke in the horse herself. I think it's good training for a child because in training a horse you train yourself.

Teilhard de Chardin

Object and subject marry and mutually transform each other in the act of knowledge; and from now on man willy-nilly finds his own image stamped on all he looks at.

Minor White

Close the circle from the features of my inner landscape, I relate, take part, participate when I close the circle of joy. Image and I united, *joyous.*

Seeing consists of attending to one thing at a time in our visual field and ignoring others. What we attend to at any one time is called figure and what we ignore is called ground. We cannot see both figure and ground at the same time but we can shift from one to the other.

Rasheed bin Fouad

No environment is perceptible because it saturates the whole field of attention. One can perceive it only after alienation — after some degree of alienation.

Edmund Carpenter

It is only when the figure has emerged from the ground and developed into a contoured whole that attachment of meaning, naming, and consequent changes in what is perceived can occur.

N.F. Dixon

Look at any landscape photograph. You see the shape of things, the mountains and trees and buildings, but not the sky.

Kurt Koffka

Dynamic interaction in the field decides what becomes a unit, what is excluded from it, what is figure, and what falls back as mere ground.

Wolfgang Kohler

Though clay may be molded into a vase, the utility of the vase lies in what is not there.

Lao-Tze

An intention is a turning of one's attention toward

Rollo May

something. In this sense, perception is directed by intentionality. This can be illustrated by the fact that consciousness consists of a figure-ground constellation. If I look at the tree, the mountain is a background; if I look at the mountain, the reverse is the case: the mountain then becomes the figure and the rest the foreground.

Floyd Ratliff

Artists who endeavor to portray the essence of real things seem to recognize almost instinctively that outline and contour are of paramount importance. The primitive artist, limited by crude methods, seems content to show what is of utmost significance to him.

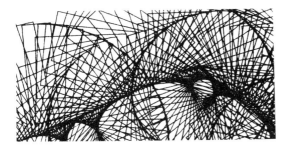

The word Gestalt comes from the German and has
the approximate meaning of shape, form configuration, pattern. In terms of design it means
that the "whole is different from the sum of its
parts." A picture made up from a mosaic of tile
parts is much different from the individual tiles
that make up the picture — the whole. The picture
has shape, form pattern, meaning.

*Rasheed bin
Fouad*

This thou must always bear in mind, what is the
nature of the whole, and what is thy nature, and
how this is related to that, and what kind of a part
it is of what kind of a whole; and that there is no
one who hinders thee from always doing and
saying the things which are according to the nature
of which thou art a part.

Marcus Aurelius

This recognition, in real life, of a rhythm of
surfaces, lines, and values is for me the essence of
photography; composition should be a constant of
preoccupation, being a simultaneous coalition —
an organic coordination of visual elements.

*Henri
Cartier-Bresson*

Although the biological machine can be analyzed
piece by piece, humanness cannot be understood
by reducing man to something less than human
and ignoring the complexities which make for the

Gestalt

Rene Dubos   unique richness of his life.

Paul Klee   Abstract formal elements are put together like numbers and letters to make concrete beings or abstract things; in the end a formal cosmos is achieved so much like the creation that a mere breath suffices to transform religion into art.

Wolfgang Kohler   A melody or a chord is played on a piano. A person who is at all musical can immediately recognize it as belonging to the major or minor mode. We would try in vain to explain such a whole quality in terms of the notes taken in isolation and their separate properties. Neither the major nor the minor character can be found in isolated notes...

Abraham Maslow   But this is precisely what the great artist does. He is able to bring together clashing colors, forms that fight each other, dissonances of all kinds, into a unity. And this is also what the great theorist does when he puts puzzling and inconsistent facts together so that we can see that they really belong together. And so also for the great statesman, the great therapist, the great philosopher, the great parent, the great inventor. They are all integrators, able to bring separates and even opposites together into unity.

Max Planck   In modern mechanics merely local relations are not sufficient for a formulation of the laws of motion; we do not obtain an adequate formulation of the laws until we regard the physical system as a whole.

Minor White   Before he has seen the whole, how unusually perceptive and imaginative the person must be to evolve the entire sequence by meditating on its single, pair, or triplet of essential images.

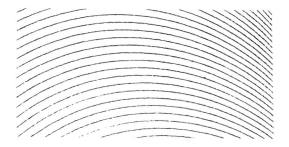

The interval invites participation: it creates riddles that involve one.

Edmund Carpenter

In the West, man perceives the objects but not the spaces between. In Japan, the spaces are perceived, named, and revered as the MA, or intervening interval.

Edward Hall

If we listen to a continuous note on the fringe of audibility, the sound seems to stop at regular intervals and then start again. Such oscillations are due to a periodic decrease and increase in one's attention, not to any change in the note.

Carl Jung

Touch as interval has never been properly investigated. By an interval in music is meant the difference in pitch between any two notes. The great variety of intervals experienced in touch carries the signals to the brain, which gives them meaning. As in music, so also in tactile experience, intervals can be either concordant or discordant. The psychophysics of the subject has yet to be investigated.

Ashley Montagu

Paramount to all this, is my awareness of the value of silence. Mozart said at one point, that he wasn't so much interested in notes as the space between them. He seemed to be intuitively aware of the Japanese belief that all action occurs in the

Interval

Harley Parker vacuum, all action occurs in the space between events.

Henry Thoreau Fishermen, hunters, wood-choppers and others, spending their lives in the fields and woods, in a peculiar sense a part of Nature themselves, are often in a more favorable mood for observing her, in the intervals of their pursuits, than philosophers or poets even, who approach her with expectation.

Minor White A sequence of photographs is like a cinema of stills. The time and space between photographs is filled by the beholder, first of all from himself, then from what he can read in the implications of design, the suggestions springing from treatment, and any symbolism that might grow from within the subject itself.

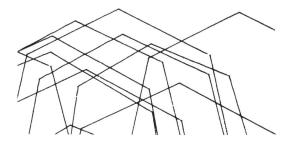

Isomorphism literally refers to the similarity of forms. In Gestalt psychology is was used to establish a hypothesis that there is a correspondence of some kind between the stimulus information in the visual field and the excitation it causes in the cerebral cortex.

Rasheed bin Fouad

Representation consists in creating, with the means of a particular medium an equivalent of a perceptual concept...whatever the medium, there will be structural similarities of the representation and perceptual concept. Such structural similarity of configuration in different media has been termed isomorphism in Gestalt theory.

Rudolf Arnheim

The emotional colors and drives of the inner life become tangible when the artist can create or discover a corresponding form.

Graham Collier

The shaping of personality through responses to environmental stimuli has an anatomical basis in the brain's structure, because functional stimulation activates structural development in the nervous system. Anatomically, as well as intellectually, the brain develops with use and wastes away with disuse.

Rene Dubos

The tactile sensation of wetness is composed of that of coldness and that of smoothness of surface.

Isomorphism

Hermann Helmholtz

Consequently, on inadvertently touching a cold piece of smooth metal, we often get the impression of having touched something wet.

Wolfgang Kohler

Merely GEOMETRICAL relations between local events in the brain have no importance whatever for structure of experienced space. This structure depends altogether upon FUNCTIONAL relationships.

Ulric Neisser

Merely *geometrical* relations between local events in the brain have no importance whatever for structure of experienced space. This structure depends altogether upon *functional* relationships.

Minor White

Not equal to
Not metaphor
Not standing for
Not sign

equivalent to
equivalence
but being also
but direct connection to
invisible Resonance.

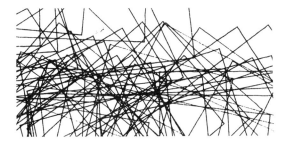

Perceptual defense is part of the general defense mechanism man uses to ward off anxiety. It refers to the ability of the perceptual system to intercept and dismiss potentially unpleasant stimuli before they come into awareness. Since this happens below the level of awareness or consciousness it is subliminal.

Rasheed bin Fouad

...perceptual defense — the manner in which organisms utilize their perceptual readiness to ward off events that are threatening, but about which there is nothing they can do.

Jerome Bruner

Of all the phenomena discussed in this book, perceptual defense is by far the most important, not so much in itself, but rather because of its implications...that consciousness depends upon a system in parallel with that subserving behavior, and that the organism can receive, process, and transmit information which has no representation in consciousness, at any stage of its passage.

N.F. Dixon

Repression may prevent a person from seeing something that is in plain view, or distort that which he does see, or falsify the information coming in through the sense organs, in order to protect the ego from apprehending an object that is dangerous or that is associated with a danger that would arouse anxiety.

Calvin Hall

Perceptual Defense

Wilson Bryan Key

Considered the central mechanism of perceptual defense, repression is probably the most significant technique by which humans avoid dealing with reality. This would generally involve the barring or censoring of memories, feelings, or perceptions with high anxiety-producing potential.

Wilson Bryan Key

Perceptions that somehow threaten the individual, or that he finds difficult to consciously handle, are subject to being sidetracked from the conscious into the unconscious. Humans defend themselves in this way from perceptual damage which might result if this inhibitory mechanism did not operate.

Rollo May

Apathy and lack of feeling are also defenses against anxiety. When a person continually faces dangers he is powerless to overcome, his final line of defense is at last to avoid even feeling the dangers.

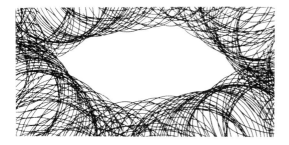

Personal space refers to the psychological distance between two or more people or between a person and an object such as a photograph, sculpture, painting and the like. Every person requires a certain distance between himself and another or an object in order to feel at ease. When personal space is violated we become tense and defensive.

Rasheed bin Fouad

Without the participant's being necessarily aware of it, *human beings are constantly engaged in adjustments to the presence and activities of other human beings.*

Ray Birdwhistell

A basic belief common to both pre- and postliterate men is that powers reside in all things; words, objects, songs and particularly, people. Under certain circumstances, these unfold themselves or are released creating change, especially when they transact with energies emanating from other properties.

Edmund Carpenter

Spatial changes give a tone to a communication, accent it, and at times even override the spoken word. The flow and shift of distance between people as they interact with each other is part and parcel of the communication process.

Edward Hall

For the artist, dialogue with nature remains a *sine qua non*. The artist is a man, himself nature, and a

Personal Space

Paul Klee　part of nature within a natural space.

Desmond Morris　We carry with us, everywhere we go, a portable territory called Personal Space. If people move inside this space, we feel threatened. If they keep too far outside it, we feel rejected. The result is a subtle series of spatial adjustments, usually operating quite unconsciously and producing ideal compromises as far as possible.

Susan Sontag　Between photographer and subject, there has to be distance. The camera doesn't rape or even possess, though it may presume, intrude, trespass, distort, exploit, and at the farthest reach of methaphor, assassinate....

Minor White　Creativity with portraits involves the invocation of a state of rapport when only a camera stands between two people...mutual vulnerability and mutual trust.

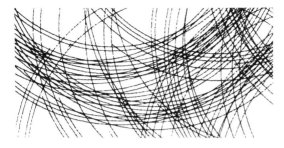

If we can use the term "redundancy" without the
normative judgement of unnecessary, superfluous,
extravagant, emptily repetitive, nonfunctioning
signals, it will focus attention upon the richness of
the communicative process.   *Ray Birdwhistell*

The five modes of attention, listening, smelling,
tasting, touching, and looking, are specialized in
one respect and unspecialized in another. They are
specialized for vibration, odor, chemical contact,
mechanical contact, and ambient light, respec-
tively, but they are redundant for the information
in these energies whenever it overlaps.   *James Gibson*

Like all good communication services, our senses
rarely take chances with one signal alone. They
make use of what engineers call "redundancies,"
the mutual confirmation of messages by repetition
and cross reference.   *E.H. Gombrich*

Many of the organs of the body are duplicated,
but the eyes, and the ears, are unusual in working
in close co operation; for they share and compare
information, so that together they perform feats
impossible for the single eye or ear.   *Richard Gregory*

Many of the Gestalt principles of perceptual
organization pertain essentially to the distribution
of information in the picture. For example "good"

Redundancy

Ralph Haber

figure is a figure with a high degree of internal redundancy. Any given part is predictable from previously seen parts.

Edward Hall

All organisms are highly dependent on redundancy; that is, information received from one system is backed up by other systems in case of failure.

George Miller

It has been estimated that English sentences are about 75 percent redundant: that is, about four times as long as they would need to be if we used our alphabet with maximum efficiency.

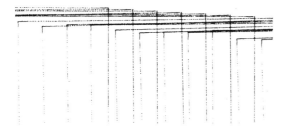

Indian music is not learned by reading notes, but
by listening to the playing of the teacher and thus
developing a feeling for the music, just as the T'ai
Chi movements are not learned by verbal in-
structions but by doing them over and over again
in unison with the teacher.   *Fritjof Capra*

Newspapers are mirrors; a few even call themselves that. They reflect their readers. Their
repeat/repeat of cliche is closer to incantation than
to communication.   *Edmund Carpenter*

[It is] a general rule of the processes of our
memory, that impressions frequently repeated in
the same manner and always united in the same
kind of connection, under otherwise similar circumstances leave a much more enduring trace of
themselves and their relationships, and are recalled
to consciousness much more surely and readily in
this combination than those which have occurred   *Hermann*
to us only in casual and changing relationships.   *Helmholtz*

How many times do you think a person should see
a movie to catch everything in it...Three times, at
least, to pick out all the details and the intentions
behind them.   *Alfred Hitchcock*

The dance transforms man's innate passive rhythm
into active rhythm of personal music. Dancing

Repetition

Joost Meerloo

changes mechanical repetitiousness into passionate life.

George Miller

Rehearsal or repetition has the very important effect of organizing many separate items into a single unit, thus reducing the load our memory must carry and leaving us free for further thinking.

Robert Ornstein

Each of the major Eastern traditions — Buddhism, Yoga, Sufism — uses exercises involving different sensory modalities. A chant is repeated in the various traditions: a word, koan, mantra, prayer, or dervish call....It seems that the sensory mode of meditation makes little difference. The important effect is the state evoked by the process of repetition.

Minor White

I must take care to sequence fully and clearly so that repetitions and variations will help insight.

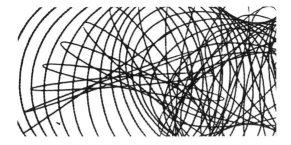

The cerebral cortex of the brain consists of a right
and left hemisphere joined together by a large
bundle of some two million interconnecting nerve
fibers called the corpus callosum. The right
hemisphere tends to be intuitive in its operation
and is connected to the left side of the body while
the left hemisphere tends to be rational and is
connected to the right side of the body.

*Rasheed bin
Fouad*

Since childhood, I have been enchanted by the fact
and the symbolism of the right hand and the left
— the one the doer, the other the dreamer. The
right is order and lawfulness, *le droit*...Of the left
hand we say that it is awkward...

Jerome Bruner

The contrast of yin and yang is not only the basic
ordering principle throughout Chinese culture, but
is also reflected in the two dominant trends of
Chinese thought. Confucianism was rational,
masculine, active and dominating. Taoism, on the
other hand, emphasized all that was intuitive,
feminine, mystical, and yielding.

Fritjof Capra

The real power of music is its ability to go past the
intellectual part of our minds to some other region
that moves us and reaches part of us that we were
not in contact with before. So it's not necessary
that you understand a song intellectually; it's more
important that you feel it, and that it touches you

Neil Diamond

in some way that you may not understand. I think that's the ideal response and reaction to a song.

Ecclesiastes

The heart of a wise man is in his right hand, and the heart of a fool is in his left hand.

Iroquois Indian Myth

Twin brothers grew up representing two ways of the world which are in all people. The twins were identified as right-handed and left-handed, straight mind and crooked mind, upright and devious.

Carl Jung

I had always been impressed by the fact that there are a surprising number of individuals who never use their minds if they can avoid it, and an equal number who do use their minds, but in an amazingly stupid way. I was also surprised to find many intelligent and wide-awake people who lived...as if they had never learned to use their sense organs...

Robert Ornstein

The left hemisphere (connected to the right side of the body) is predominately involved with analytic, logical thinking, especially in verbal and mathematical functions. Its mode of operation is primarily linear...the right hemisphere...seems specialized for holistic mentation. Its language ability is quite limited. This hemisphere is primarily responsible for our orientation in space, artistic endeavor, crafts, body image, recognition of faces.

Henry Thoreau

It is impossible for the same person to see things from the poet's point of view and that of the man of science.

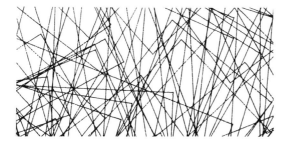

Sensory deprivation refers to a situation in which a person is isolated from his environment for a period of time. He is deprived of sight, sound, smell, touch and taste stimuli. In a few hours he feels quite uncomfortable and after several hours begins to hallucinate. The experience is extremely disruptive to the human psyche and to the perceptual system. Man cannot exist in isolation.

Rasheed bin Fouad

Without information on what is going on in time and space the brain cannot work....Evidently then the mind, in order to cope with the world, must fulfill two functions. It must gather information and it must process it.

Rudolf Arnheim

Some people experience hallucinations, as well as a general falling off in their ability to concentrate or solve problems, after hours or days of isolation. It seems that the sensory system requires a more or less continuous stream of information or it starts to go off on its own, as in extreme fatigue or under the action of certain drugs such as opium or lysergic acid.

Richard Gregory

Therefore if you desire to discover your soul, withdraw your thoughts from outward and material things, forgetting, if possible, your own body and its five senses.

Walter Hilton

Sensory Deprivation

Cultural as well as individual existence depends on perceiving, and modes of thinking about perceiving are central in setting the intellectual climate of any time. In fact, to be alive is to be sentient. If we did not perceive, each one of us would be alone in a deeply profound sense of the term, if indeed we could be considered to exist at all.

William Ittelson

Yet in order to sustain his creed, contemporary man pays the price in a remarkable lack of introspection. He is blind to the fact that, with all his rationality and efficiency, he is possessed by "powers" that are beyond his control. His gods and demons have not disappeared at all; they have merely got new names.

Carl Jung

Media-induced sensory deprivation among millions of media audiences may already have launched at least part of modern society on the road to neurosis and psychosis. We now have an entire generation whose sense of touch has been starved.

Wilson Bryan Key

Speech is civilization itself. The word, even the most contradictory word, preserves contact — it is silence which isolates.

Thomas Mann

...ill effects of maternal deprivation...are probably the result of perceptual deprivations, principally tactile, visual, and probably vestibular.

Ashley Montagu

No matter the form or technique, the essence of meditation seems to consist in an attempt to restrict awareness to a single unchanging source of stimulation for a definite period of time.

Robert Ornstein

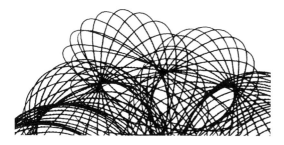

The text was written with reading aloud in mind.
That cannot be recommended; but it is suggested
that the reader attend with his ear to what he
takes off the page: for variations of tone, pace,
shape, and dynamics are here particularly
unavailable to the eye alone, and with their loss, a
good deal of meaning escapes.

*James Agee and
Walker Evans*

Communication, upon investigation, appears to be
a system which makes use of the channels of all
the sensory modalities. By this model, communication is a continuous process utilizing the
various channels and the combinations of them as
appropriate to the particular situation.

Ray Birdwhistell

What we generally mean when we speak of
representation or veridicality it that perception is
predictive in varying degrees. That is to say, the
object that we see can also be felt and smelled and
there will somehow be a match or a congruity
between what we see, feel and smell.

Jerome Bruner

In the tribal world, the eye listens, the ear sees and
all the senses assist each other in concert, in a
many-layered symphony of the senses, a cinematic
flow which includes our "five and country senses."

Edmund Carpenter

The living animal is stimulated not only from

sources in the environment but also by itself. Its internal organs provide stimulation, and so do the movements of its extremities and sense organs or feelers, and the locomotor movements of its whole body through space.

James Gibson

The seeing of objects involves many sources of information beyond those meeting the eye when we look at an object. It generally involves knowledge of the object derived from previous experience, and this experience is not limited to vision but may include the other senses; touch, taste, smell, hearing and perhaps also temperature and pain.

Richard Gregory

The shape and form and space of the outer world of reality, its figures and the background from which they emerge are gradually built by the infant out of the building blocks of its experience, entering through all its senses, always contingent, correlated, measured, and evaluated by the criterion of touch.

Ashley Montagu

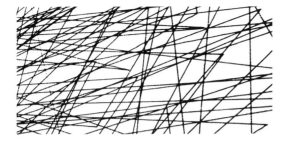

The word limen means threshold and the word subliminal means below threshold. Subliminal perception refers to stimuli which are below our threshold for awareness, do not influence us consciously but can influence us unconsciously. The threshold level for awareness varies from one person to another and also varies according to one's psychological mood.

Rasheed bin Fouad

Impulses occurring in the daytime, if they are not very great and powerful, pass unnoticed because of greater waking impulses. But in the time of sleep the opposite takes place; for then small impulses seem to be great.

Aristotle

Much is perceptible which is not perceived by us.

Democritus

Complex arrays of visual information can be read into the nervous system and produce subsequent effects without ever achieving phenomenal representation.

N.F. Dixon

We all see, hear, smell and taste many things without noticing them at the time, either because our attention is deflected or because the stimulus to our senses is too slight to leave a conscious impression. The unconscious, however, has taken note of them, and such subliminal sense per-

Subliminal

Carl Jung

ceptions play a significant part in our everyday lives.

Wilson Bryan Key

Hidden anatomical details play an important role in art. The mind unconsciously, apparently, assimilates and structures unseen portions of the anatomy in a search for meaning. A sculpture's deeper meaning is often communicated through what is not seen but is logically there, the perception passing only into the viewer's unconscious.

Gottfried Wilheim Leibnitz

There are numberless perceptions, little noticed, which are not sufficiently distinguished to be perceived or remembered, but which become known through certain consequences.

Marshall McLuhan

Environments by reason of their total character are mostly subliminal to ordinary experience.

Minor White

This unexpected image was the record of an inner state that I did not remember seeing and he did not remember experiencing at the moment of exposure.

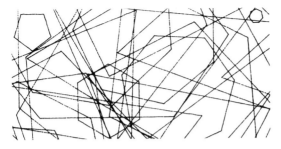

Synesthesia describes an experience in which
stimuli from one sensory mode influences that of
another. A person listening attentively to music
can have a visual experience of colors. One can see
colors with his ears and feel texture with his eyes.
An effective photography of food is one that
makes you drool. The senses are all in-
terconnected.

*Rasheed bin
Fouad*

It was Impressionists who reminded us that the
world contained "bodies": total, integrated. They
allowed us to pick up that apple, see — smell —
taste — swallow it. They broke with the nonin-
volved visual world.

Edmund Carpenter

The feeling occasioned by running the fingers over
sand-paper is not unlike that experienced by
hearing the filing of a saw.

John Dewey

In sight, as in hearing, there is very little of *im-
mediate* emotional quality. This very fact, of
course, indefinitely enlarges the range of emotions
which visual sensations take on through their
indirect connections.

John Dewey

What is called "synesthesia," the splashing over of
impressions from one sense modality to another, is
a fact to which all languages testify...We speak of
loud colors or bright sounds...There is touch in

119

Synesthesia

E.H. Gombrich

such terms as "velvety voice" and "cold night," taste with "sweet harmonies" of colors or sound, and so on through countless permutations.

Edward Hall

Touch and visual spatial experiences are so interwoven that the two cannot be separated.

Paul Klee

The eye like a grazing animal feels its way over the surface.

Ernst Mach

Colors, sounds, temperatures, pressures, spaces, times, and so forth, are connected with one another in manifold ways; and with them are associated dispositions of mind, feeling, and volitions.

Ashley Montagu

It is much more important to experience tactile and auditory stimulations in the early developing years than it is to experience visual ones. As soon, however, as one has developed through one's tactile and auditory senses the know-how of being human, vision becomes by far the most important of the senses. Yet a vision can only become meaningful on the basis of what it has felt and what it has heard.

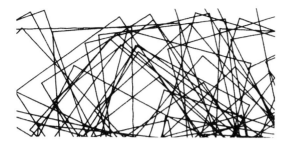

With sight and hearing, we experience things
outside of us; with taste and smell, only restricted
parts of us are affected. But touch we feel inside:
when we encounter an object, it resists, presses
back, and thus we learn that the world is composed of other bodies. If it weren't for this, we
would move through the world like phantoms.

Edmund
Carpenter

Let us begin to paint as if we held things in our
hands, not as if we were looking at them at all.

Paul Cezanne

...if we attempt to analyze our mental images to
discover their primary constituents, we will find
them composed of sense data derived from vision
and from memories of touch and movement.

E.H. Gombrich

Texture...is appraised and appreciated almost
entirely by touch, even when it is visually
presented. With few exceptions...it is the memory
of tactile experiences that enables us to appreciate
texture.

Edward Hall

When we inquire about the empirical conditions
under which the concept of space is developed, we
must consider chiefly the tactile sense, since blind
persons can develop a complete concept of space
without the aid of vision.

Hermann
Helmholtz

If humans could be said to possess one basic

Touch

Wilson Bryan Key

sensory input that supplies the brain with information, it would involve *touching* — the
sensation or experience of tactility. A human
simply could not adjust and survive without
touching. This could include both actual contact
touching and touching by *synesthesia,* whereby
touching can be experienced visually or via
another sensory input.

Ashley Montagu

The tactile quality of vision is apparent in the
touching of another with the eyes. Hence one
avoids looking or staring at strangers, except in
certain conventionally accepted situations.

Proverb

Seeing is believing but to touch is the word of
God.

St. Thomas

Unless I see in his hands the print of the nails, and
put my finger into the place of the nails, and put
my hand into his side, I will not believe.

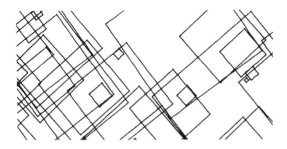

Literally thousands of experiences teach us unconsciously that space communicates.

Edward Hall

As a general rule, the unconscious aspect of any event is revealed to us in dreams, where it appears not as rational thought but as a symbolic image.

Carl Jung

Part of the unconscious consists of a multitude of temporarily obscured thoughts, impressions, and images that, in spite of being lost, continue to influence our conscious minds.

Carl Jung

Much, if not most, of significant human thought operates in this strange wilderness of the unconscious mind. The unconscious apparently does not simply perceive *things,* but somehow perceives *the meaning of things.* Unconscious thought processes have long been believed to be the source of man's creative ability, perhaps the source of all his innovations.

Wilson Bryan Key

Art plays an *unknowing* game with ultimate things, and yet achieves them!

Paul Klee

There can be no unprejudiced eye for the simple reason that vision is full of ambiguities, and all perception...is an inferential construction which proceeds on various levels, and most of it unconsciously.

Arthur Koestler

Unconscious

Abraham Maslow

The essential word is *courage* — nerve, brass, chutzpah — at least for opening one's mouth and even more for committing yourself to print. Of course *everybody* functions by intuition in part, or at least everybody has this possibility. Many don't dare to express it (even though they act on it), but I suppose there are many who don't even let it become conscious and who think of the "wild surmise" as a trap, a danger, an inner whisper from the devil.

Rollo May

Neurotic problems are the language of the unconscious emerging into social awareness.

Minor White

Sequences originate for me from some hidden place. Though I habitually play photographs against each other, or words against images in pairs, triplets, or rows of four with expectations of magic, sequences originate from within. And I prefer to let them. In fact I cannot seriously do otherwise than photograph on impulse and let whatever words will, flow spontaneously.

Agee, J. and Evans, W. **Let Us Now Praise Famous Men**
New York: Ballatine Books, 1972.

Arnheim, R. **Toward a Psychology of Art**
Berkeley, California: University of California Press, 1972.

Arnheim, R. **Visual Thinking**
Berkeley, California: University of California Press, 1972.

Berenson, B. **Aesthetics and History in the Visual Arts**
New York: Pantheon, 1948.

Birdwhistell, R.L. **Kinesics and Content**
Philadelphia: University of Pennsylvania Press, 1970.

Bower, T. **Development in Infancy**
San Francisco: W.H. Freeman, 1974.

Brill, A.A. **The Basic Writings of Sigmund Freud**
New York: The Modern Library, 1938.

Bruner, J. **On Knowing**
Cambridge: Harvard University Press, 1962.

Bruner, J. **Beyond the Information Given**
New York: Norton, 1973.

Camus, A. **Notebooks, 1942-1951**
New York: Alfred Knopf, 1965.

Capra, F. **The Tao of Physics**
New York: Bantam Books, 1977.

Carpenter, E. **They Became What They Beheld**
New York: E.P. Dutton, 1970.

Collier, B. **Art and the Creative Consciousness**
New Jersey: Prentice-Hall, 1972.

Cooper, H. **A House in Space**
New York: Holt, Rinehart and Winston, 1976.

De Cock, L. (ed.) **Wynn Bullock: Photography A Way of Life**
Dobbs Ferry: Morgan and Morgan, 1974.

Dewey, J. **Psychology: The Early Works 1882-1898**
Carbondale, Ill.: Southern University Press, 1967.

Dixon, N.F. **Subliminal Perception, The Nature of the Controversy**
London: McGraw-Hill, 1971.

Dubos, R. **So Human an Animal**
New York: Scribners, 1968.

Dubos, R. **A God Within**
New York: Scribners, 1972.

Eisley, L. **The Night Country**
New York: Scribners, 1971.

Ermerson, R.W. **Essays**
London: The Doves Press, 1906.

Evans, R. **An Introduction to Color**
New York: John Wiley and Sons, 1948.

Evans, R. **Eye, Film, and Camera in Color Photography**
New York: John Wiley and Sons, 1960.

Ferris, A. (ed.) **The Spiritual Sayings of Kahlil Gibran**
New York: The Citadel Press, 1962.

Festinger, L. **"Cognitive Dissonance"**
Scientific American, October, 1962.

Fouad, Rasheed bin
(Private Communication, 1979)

Frankl, V. **Man's Search for Meaning**
New York: Washington Square Press, 1968.

Fromm, E. **Psycholanalysis and Religion**
New York: Bantam Books, 1967.

Geelhaar, C. **Paul Klee and the Bauhaus**
Greenwich, Conn.: New Graphic Society, 1973.

Gibson, H.H. **The Senses Considered as Perceptual Systems**
Boston: Houghton Mifflin, 1966.

Gombrich, E.H. **Art and Illusion**
Princeton, New Jersey: Princeton University Press, 1969.

Gombrich, E.H. **"The Visual Image"**
Scientific American, September, 1972.

Gregory, R. **Eye and Brain**
New York: McGraw-Hill, 1966.

Haber, R. **"How We Remember What We See"**
Scientific American, May, 1970.

Haber, R. and Hershenson, R. **The Psychology of Visual Perception**
New York: Rinehart and Winston, Inc., 1973.

Hall, C.A. **A Primer of Freudian Psychology**
New York: The World Publishing Co., 1954.

Hall, E. **The Hidden Dimension**
New York: Doubleday, 1966.

Hammerskjold, D. **Markings**
New York: Alfred Knopf, 1964.

Henle, M. (ed.) **The Selected Papers of Wolfgang Kohler**
New York: Liverright, 1971.

Ittelson, W. **Environment and Cognition**
New York: Seminar Press, 1973.

James, W.J. **Psychology**
New York: Henry Holt and Co., 1948.

Johnson, A.H. (ed.) **The Wit and Wisdom of John Dewey**
New York: Beacon, 1949.

Jung, C.G. **Man and His Symbols**
New York: Doubleday, 1971.

Key, W.B. **Subliminal Seduction**
New York: New American Library, 1973.

Klee, F. (ed.) **The Diaries of Paul Klee, 1898-1918**
University of California Press, 1964.

Klee, P. **Paul Klee, Watercolors, Drawings, Paintings**
New York: Abrams, 1969.

Koestler, A. **The Act of Creation**
New York: MacMillan, 1964.

Kohler, W. **The Task of Gestalt Psychology**
Princeton, New Jersey: Princeton University Press, 1969.

Lawrence, D.H. **Phoenix**
New York: Viking, 1972.

Mann, T. **The Magic Mountain**
New York: Random House, 1969.

Maslow, A. **Toward a Psychology of Being**
New York: D. Van Nostrand, 1969.

Maslow, B. **Abraham H. Maslow: A Memorial Volume**
Monterey, California: Brooks/Cole, 1972.

May, R. **Love and Will**
New York: Norton, 1969.

May, R. **Power and Innocence**
New York: Norton, 1972.

Meerloo, J. **The Dance**
New York: Chilton Company, 1960.

Merton, T. **Conjectures of a Guilty Bystander**
Garden City, New York: Doubleday, 1966.

Miller, G. **The Psychology of Communications**
New York: Penguin Books, 1969.

Montagu, A. **Touching: The Human Significance of Skin**
New York: Harper and Row, 1971.

Morrie, D. **Manwatching**
New York: Abrams, 1977.

Neisser, U. **Cognitive Psychology**
New York: Appleton-Century-Crofts, 1967.

Neisser, U. **"The Process of Vision"**
Scientific American, September, 1968.

Ornstein, R. **The Psychology of Consciousness**
New York: Penguin Books, 1975.

Piaget, J. **Psychology of Intelligence**
Totowa, New Jersey: Littlefield, Adams, and Co., 1966.

Ratliff, F. **Mach Bands**
San Francisco: Holden-Day, Inc., 1965.

Saint-Exupery, A. **The Little Prince**
New York: Harcourt, Brace and World, Inc., 1971.

Shahn, B. **The Shape of Content**
Cambridge: Harvard University Press, 1957.

Sontag, B. **On Photography**
New York: Farrar, Straus and Giroux, 1978.

Spitz, R. **The First Year of Life**
New York: International University Press, 1965.

Sullivan, H. **Conceptions of Modern Psychiatry**
New York: W.W. Norton, 1953.

Teilhard de Chardin, P. **The Phenomen of Man**
New York: Harper and Brothers, 1959

Thoreau, H. **The Writings of Henry David Thoreau**
Boston: Houghton Mifflin, 1906.

White, M. **Mirrors, Messages and Manifestations**
Millerton, New York: Aperture, 1969.

Williams, O. (ed.) **The Pocketbook of Modern Verse**
New York: Pocket Books, Inc., 1954.

Youngblood, G. **Expanded Cinema**
New York: E.P. Dutton and Co., 1970.

Zabel, M.D. **The Portable Henry James**
New York: Viking Press, 1971.

My sincere thanks to the authors and publishers listed in this section and in the bibliography for the use of their copyrighted material.

Let Us Now Praise Famous Men by James Agee and Walker Evans © renewed 1969 by Mia Fritsch Agee. Used by permission of the publisher, Houghton Mifflin Company.

Toward a Psychology of Art and **Visual Thinking** by Rudolf Arnheim © 1966 and 1969 by the Regents of the University of California. Reprinted by the permission of the University of California Press.

Aesthetics and History in the Visual Arts by Bernard Berenson © 1948 by Pantheon Books, a Division of Random House.

Beyond the Given Information, Studies in the Psychology of Knowing, Selected and Edited by Jeremy M. Anglin, with the permission of W.W. Norton & Company, Inc. Copyright © 1973 by Jerome S. Bruner and Jeremy M. Anglin.

On Knowing: Essays for the Left Hand by Jerome Bruner, copyright © 1962 by the President and Fellows of Harvard College. Used by permission of Harvard University Press.

They Became What They Beheld by Edmund Carpenter and Ken Heyman, copyright © 1970 by Edmund Carpenter and Ken Heyman. Published by Outerbridge and Dienstfrey. By permission of E.P. Dutton.

The Tao of Physics by Fritjof Capra. Copyright © 1975 by Fritjof Capra, Shambhala Publications Inc., the U.S. publishers and Wildwood House, the British publishers.

The illustrations are computer drawings programmed
by the designer and drawn by a Zeta Incremental
Digital Plotter.

Book design by Donald Harbison
Production by Connie Shermer
Typesetting by Courier-Journal Graphics,
    Rochester, NY in Paladium and Helvetica
Printed by Tucker Printers, Rochester, NY
    on Mohawk Vellum #70 Cream White and
    Monadnock Caress Velvet #80
Bound at Wm F. Zahrndt & Sons, Inc.